INTEGRITY THERAPY

integrity therapy

john w. drakeford

A NEW DIRECTORY
IN PSYCHOTHERAPY

BROADMAN PRESS

Nashville, Tennessee

TO
O. HOBART MOWRER

If Diogenes, lamp in hand, had met him in his
search for an honest man, the quest would have
been at an end.

DEWEY DECIMAL CLASSIFICATION NUMBER: 253.5

Library of Congress catalog card number: 67-19396

Printed in the United States of America

2.5D696

CONTENTS

1

REDISCOVERY OF AN OLD IDEA

Promptly at twelve noon John Harris entered the hotel banquet hall for the civic club meeting. Popular with his fellow club members, the middle-aged clergyman exchanged greetings on the way to his seat. He approached Dr. Salzek, a successful but somewhat irascible psychiatrist with, "Hi, Doc! Got enough business these days?"

"More than I can handle," came the response, "and I wouldn't be worked to death if it weren't for you preachers, threatening people with hell fire and building up their guilt."

Harris replied with a wave of his hand and went on his way, a smiling face hiding the inner turmoil. Trying desperately to stay current with the latest developments in the behavioral sciences, and applying them to his work, he was committed to helping his fellows. The accusation of being a purveyor of guilt struck home hard.

Not only his message but his total role is being reevaluated by the modern minister who is earnestly trying to carry on his pastoral work in a scientific age. One of the most potent sources of his conflict lies in deciding just what should be his response to the many people who track to his study door or the unfortunate maladjusted folk he stumbles upon in the course of his pastoral calling.

A national survey revealed that 42 percent of the people facing emotional difficulties turn to their minister when trials come.

In so doing, they are following a historical precedent, for from time immemorial people in trouble have turned to their religious guide or mentor when seeking a way out of emotional difficulties.

The problem is that although these statistics reveal that common, everyday people still have at least some recognition of this important role of the pastor, he himself is having second thoughts about his own capabilities and responsibilities. He has tried to upgrade himself by concentrating on his preaching, on church administration, or on community activities. But people with personal problems continue to bother him. He is stuck with his role, no matter how inadequate he feels or how much he tries to hand it over to someone else.

Fortuitously today's minister is well educated and knows there is good specialized, professional help available for those who need it. In the past, ministers had more than a lurking fear that psychiatrists were meddling with their parishioners' moral and religious convictions. The psychiatrists were just as apprehensive that the clergyman might be "doing therapy." But now has come a truce and the happy announcement that psychiatry and religion are reconciled.

Even with the accomplishment of this historic reconciliation, at least some of the clergy are having second thoughts. They are asking themselves whether it was really a reconciliation or just a plain surrender. When the church member enters therapy the psychiatrist may commence by warning him about his religion, the hazards of its repressive demands, and above all, the danger of a well-developed sense of guilt. The patient may even be advised to, at least temporarily, quit practicing his religion because such archaic ideas are a threat to his mental health. Upon hearing of such advice, the minister swallows over and acknowledges that his psychiatric colleague is probably right. Then he mentally speculates as to whether he should not spend more time at the golf course or working for the United Givers Fund.

One of the features of our modern preacher's life will be attending conferences on the relationship of psychiatry and religion. Yet, almost invariably few, if any, psychiatrists are present. As one such conference met, a minister asked, "Where are the psychiatrists? I would like to look one in the eye and ask him a few questions." But, alas, eyeball contact may be delayed until he can afford the fee to consult with the psychiatrist in his office.

These conferences on psychiatry and religion, minus psychiatrists, will probably be dominated by psychiatric concepts from start to finish. If some poor, ignorant minister gets to his feet to ask a few questions about sin and guilt, a hush will probably come over the group. Then a few knowing smiles will appear, as one of the more knowledgeable clerical brethren gently puts things straight with a plaster of psychiatric jargon.

At such conferences the minister will learn to recognize his "limitations." In plain language, this euphemism means he must "refer" the troubled members of his flock to some professional person, who will be able to provide the specialized type of help they really need. One of the frequently used ways of expressing this is to say, "We never do anything that someone else can do better."

The chief lesson for the minister is to realize his own inadequacy in fulfilling the role he has played for so many years. Above everything else, he learns to refrain from activities which would raise his parishioners' guilt. Also, he learns how to help them see that they are sick and really need the help of a highly trained professional.

A Psychiatrist's Second Thoughts

Having successfully faced the problem of what to do about emotionally disturbed people, and having found a "scientific" solution, the minister is not a little disconcerted to discover that some of the highly trained experts themselves are reconsidering the presuppositions upon which they have been operating. Psychiatrist Glasser, one of the most forthright objectors to many commonly accepted ideas, sees the widely held theoretical concepts from which the psychotherapeutic world has operated as follows:

1. Conventional psychiatry believes firmly that mental illness exists, that people who suffer from it can be meaningfully classified, and that attempts should be made to treat them according to the diagnostic classification.
2. Conventional psychiatry holds that an essential part of treatment is probing into the patient's past life—searching for the psychological roots of his problem, because once the patient clearly understands these roots he can use his understanding to change his attitude toward life. From this change in attitude he can then develop more effective patterns of living which will solve his psychological difficulties.
3. Conventional psychiatry maintains that the patient must transfer to the therapist attitudes he held or still holds toward important people in his past life, people around whom his problems started. Using this concept, called transference, the therapist relives with the patient his past difficulties and then explains to him how he is repeating the same inadequate behavior with the therapist. The patient, through the therapist's interpretations of the transference behavior, gains insight into his past. His newly attained insight allows him to give up his old attitudes and to learn to relate to people in a better way, solving his problems.
4. Conventional psychotherapy, even in superficial counseling, emphasizes that if the patient is to change he must gain understanding and insight into his unconscious mind. Unconscious mental conflicts are considered more important than conscious problems; making the patient aware of them through the interpretation of transference, dreams, and free associations, and through educated psychiatric guessing, is necessary if therapy is to succeed.
5. Necessarily accompanying the conviction that mental illness exists, conventional psychiatry scrupulously avoids the problem

of morality, that is, whether the patient's behavior is right or wrong. Deviant behavior is considered a product of the mental illness, and the patient should not be held morally responsible because he is considered helpless to do anything about it. Once the illness is cured through the procedures described in Points 2, 3, and 4, the patient will then be able to behave according to the rules of society.

6. Teaching people to behave better is not considered an important part of therapy in conventional psychiatry, which holds the patients will learn better behavior themselves once they understand both the historical and unconscious sources of their problems.[1]

Glasser claims that in some form or another these concepts constitute the theoretical basis of nearly all systems of psychotherapy as we know them today and are taught almost universally in the colleges and universities of the U. S. A. and Canada.

With all the enthusiasm of a reformer rushing in to do battle with and challenge what he considers misleading and wrong, Glasser expresses himself in no uncertain terms. He disagrees with each of these traditionally accepted ideas. He questions the validity of each and every one of them. In justification of his stance he produces a battery of arguments and counterproposals in which he maintains:

1. Mental illness is not a diagnosable, treatable illness which is in some way like physical illness. If there is any type of analogy to medicine it is that of weakness, indicating that it can only be cured by strengthening the existing body to cope with the stresses of the world. The person normally called neurotic is afraid of reality, while the so-called psychotic denies reality—but the label makes little difference. In the practice of "reality therapy," all cases ranging from delinquent girls to psychotic veterans are in their condition because they have acted irresponsibly in the past and, as a result, continue to behave badly in the present.

2. It is not necessary to inquire into all the devious details of a patient's past history. (In all fairness, we should note that Carl

Rogers had also deleted this from client-centered therapy techniques years ago. But the idea has been particularly tenacious as is seen in the detailed case histories considered an integral part of most psychiatric procedures.) While research like this may be important for psychological generalizations, it really has no part in therapy. Knowledge of his past history often defeats the troubled person who sees himself as the unfortunate victim of his earlier days. This newer view says he must face the present and its responsibilities, and the starting point of all this is a change in present behavior.

3. Rejection of the periodic and changing transference experiences in which the individual lives through his attitude toward important persons in the past and sees them represented in his therapist. By contrast, reality therapy seeks a meaningful relationship in which the subject relates to the therapist as a new and separate person with a new and distinctive role.

4. Probing for the unconscious factor in the counselee's maladjustment may only, like the taking of a history, provide a justification and a rationale for what he is doing. The question often is, "Well now I know what is causing all my difficulties, what do I do about them?" Much of this is a waste of time. "Because no one lives a life where his needs are always fulfilled, it is impossible not to find a wealth of buried conflicts which, being similar to present difficulties, seem to explain a person's inability to fulfill his needs now."[2] In contrast, reality therapy insists on consideration of present activity and what is lacking in the subject's appreciation of his behavior at this moment.

5. The necessity for a moral stance, although it has been psychotherapy's proud boast that it remains completely detached and amoral. (Mowrer, commenting on Glasser, notes the "three R's" of his therapy: responsibility, reality, right and wrong.) Reality therapy claims that clients must be confronted with their behavior so that they can judge its quality by their own conceived standards and decide what to do about it. Delinquent girls who frankly justify prostitution illustrate this. When asked if they would like their own daughters to be prostitutes, almost invariably they reply with an emphatic no, thus passing judgment on their own activity.

6. In the conventional techniques of therapy the main task of

the therapist is to assist the client in gaining insight. Having gained insight, it is the counselee's responsibility to apply this to his pattern of life. Reality therapy doesn't bother too much about insight, but "we spend much time painstakingly examining the patient's daily activity and suggesting better ways for him to behave."[3] The therapist is a teacher involved in a special type of education—helping his pupil learn to live more effectively.

"We should say that in the six major areas covered, reality therapy differs markedly from conventional therapy. Reality therapy is not another variety of the same approach but a different way to work with people. The requirements of reality therapy — an intense personal involvement, facing reality and rejecting irresponsible behavior, and learning better ways to behave—bear little resemblance to conventional therapy and produce markedly different results."[4] These psychiatrically unconventional ideas have worked with delinquent girls, psychotic veterans and patients in a mental hospital.

While reality therapy has much in common with the therapy described in this book, particularly in the "Three R's" of psychotherapy, there is at least one main difference. Glasser does not stress the need for confession. It may be that his work with delinquent girls means they have been "caught up with" by society and their incarceration is itself an acknowledgment of failure, opening the way for new lessons in responsibility. Integrity therapy emphasizes that acceptance of responsibility demands openness and letting at least "significant others" know about one's failure to be a responsible individual.

An Unlikely Birthplace of a New Concept

Whatever might be the shortcomings of mental hospitals, there have been some remarkable responses from patients after periods of hospitalization. Following his discharge, Clifford Beers wrote *The Mind That Found Itself*, which met with such an enthusiastic reception that he launched, and became the first secretary of, the mental hygiene movement.

Anton T. Boisen, during his hospitalization, saw the possibilities of ministers playing a larger part in hospital life, became the first full-time chaplain of a mental hospital, and the founder of the Clinical Pastoral Education Movement. To these illustrious former mental hospital patients must be added a third, O. Hobart Mowrer, from whose hospitalization has come a new concept of psychotherapy.

Mowrer was already the author of a number of scholarly books on learning theory. Research professor at the University of Illinois and president of the American Psychological Association, in 1953, he was overtaken with a severe depression which led to a three-month hospitalization. He had previously been in psychoanalysis for seven years and "treated" by three analysts during this time. Following his hospitalization he concluded that psychoanalysis, with its emphasis on removing guilt, was wrong. Rather than being a villain, guilt, he felt, served a healthy purpose in interpsychic reaction.

This former follower of Freud reached the conclusion that the guilt which had given rise to his depression was fulfilling a useful and necessary function by reminding him of his past misdeeds. Until he discontinued concealing the shortcomings of the past, he would continue to experience discomfort and uneasiness. So he began to follow a course of "openness," telling significant people in his life about his past secrecy. This led to a new and meaningful experience and opened a vista of service to his fellowmen in which guilt was reevaluated and interpreted, not as an enemy, but as a friendly, motivating force.

As a research psychologist, Mowrer was interested in developing the theoretical foundations of his experience and testing his theories with troubled people. First, there were groups in his community. Later, he worked as professional consultant to the State Research Hospital at Galesburg, Illinois. In his work with these groups, Mowrer's co-workers were former mental hospital patients, along with seminary professors and ministers who were on sabbatical leave and working under a grant from the Eli Lilly Foundation.

The work was punctuated with constant sessions of appraisal and evaluation. Theories were tested out in group therapy and in consultation with chaplains, psychologists, and seminary professors. The results were very good, sometimes spectacular.

Dr. Mowrer, who believes there is nothing so practical as good theory, was constantly at work with quantities of material flowing from his prolific pen. His first two books in this field, *The Crisis in Psychiatry and Religion*[5] and *The New Group Therapy*,[6] were widely distributed. They stirred discussion in both religious and psychiatric circles. Other volumes are awaiting publication, but there has been considerable interest in the possibility of a simple, systematic setting forth of this theory of therapy, a task to which this volume addresses itself.

Hobart Mowrer does not suffer from a messiah complex. He insists he is only one voice among many and refuses to consider the use of his name for any system. While a group of Lilly fellows were flying in a university plane from Champaign to Galesburg, Illinois, there came an unusual consensus. It was agreed that the most descriptive title for this new direction in psychotherapy would be "integrity therapy."

The distinctives of integrity therapy can be gathered under a series of postulates:

1. Integrity therapy rejects all deterministic theories which make man a victim of heredity, environment, or any other force. Every individual is answerable for himself, and exercises his responsibility in making his personal decisions.

2. Each person has a conscience, or value system, the violation of which gives rise to guilt. This condition is not a sickness but a result of his wrongdoing and irresponsibility.

3. The typical self-defeating reaction to personal wrongdoing is concealment. In this secrecy, guilt throws up symptoms of

varying degrees of severity, from vague discomfort to complete immobilization.

4. As secrecy brought on his trouble and separated him from his fellows, so openness with "significant others" is the individual's first step on the road back to normality.

5. The process of socialization involves a group which could be called a microcosm or small world exercising both a corrective and supportive function for the growing individual.

6. Openness by itself is not enough and the individual is under an obligation to undertake some activity of restitution appropriate to his acknowledged failure in life.

7. The only way to continue as a truly authentic person is not only to remain open and make restitution but also to feel a responsibility to carry the message of integrity therapy to other needy people.

The dynamics of symptom formation and the pathway back to meaningful living may be diagramed as in Figures 1 and 2.

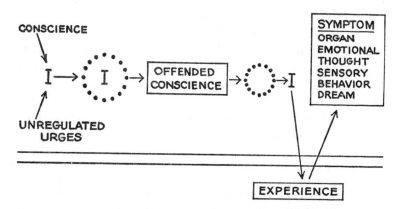

Fig. 1. The individual (I) is in a state of tension between his conscience and his unregulated urges. While he lives by his values, he is symbolically at one with his fellows. But once he fails to live by his values, he symbolically separates himself from his society. The action is internalized by repression and the unworthy experience in the unconscious throws up symptoms.

Fig. 2. The distressed individual (I) seeks help from the therapist (T) who opens his life, evoking a response of transparency. The individual is introduced to the group of "significant others" where he learns to make restitution and proceeds to become a part of the therapeutic enterprise.

New Horizons

As will be seen in the concluding chapter, integrity therapy opens a whole new field of possibility for the minister. He now discovers that his religious convictions concerning the nature of man represent the wisdom of the ages and have within them many clues to both man's hurt and healing. The minister also realizes he does not have to abandon his view of man for some allegedly enlightened therapy which may in reality be far more poetic, unreal, and wish-fulfilling than his traditional concepts.

Not only ministers but almost any perceptive and interested person can play a part in helping troubled people. Evidence has been produced to show that, even in using orthodox techniques, laymen can render a useful service. The possibilities were dramatized by the experience of counseling services in England. Faced with a shortage of trained personnel, the Marriage Guidance Movement commenced by using laymen and women. They were carefully selected, screened, and instructed. Then they set to work within a team. Possibly the most illuminating discovery came from the evaluation of the psychiatric supervisors, who, after having worked with both lay and professional groups of counselors, admitted that:

In the quality of work done there has been no differences at all between the lay counselors and the professional counselors.

They simply had to admit against their prejudices that properly trained lay counselors who were properly selected in the first place can do every bit as good a job as professional counselors.[7]

From the academic point of view these discoveries are most disconcerting, but they indicate possibilities for the utilization of laymen in the work of interpersonal relationships.

Experience in the practice of integrity therapy has shown that women with only high school education, having been in groups themselves become capable and competent leaders. The requirements are fairly simple. Basic honesty, a sensitivity to others, a willingness to study simple group techniques, and, above all, a motivating concern for others. This opens an ever-widening horizon of possibilities for lay men and women to join in a crusade to release their fellows from their prison house of despair.

One point which bothers some critics is the fear that integrity therapy may oversimplify the difficulties of life and seek to offer one simple solution for all the mental stresses of man. In response, it must be frankly acknowledged that life is so complex that there is never a single panacea for every ill.

There are obviously some situations in which integrity therapy would not be appropriate. No maladjusted individual whose trouble stems from a physical root could be helped by this therapy. Unduly suspicious personalities would experience difficulty in using a technique which calls for openness and self-revelation. People not responsible for their own lives, children living under the care of dominant parents, institutionalized persons, or older folks are not good subjects for this type of therapy.

The sociopath, with little value system for leverage, will obviously be beyond help from a normal integrity therapy group. Nevertheless, as we will later see, it may well be that the sociopath's only hope will be an intensive application of these very principles.

Like any form of psychotherapy, integrity therapy has its own inherent limitations. But these may not be as restrictive as some have imagined. Integrity therapy has a width of application that the inexperienced find difficult to understand.

The plan of this book is to consider the roots from which integrity therapy has grown and examine the primary concepts of conscience, guilt, confession, and socialization in their interrelatedness, and the healthy function of guilt in human experience. Part two presents integrity therapy techniques. The final chapter is on the application of integrity therapy to church work.

2

CONSCIENCE DOTH MAKE

Shakespeare said, "Conscience doth make cowards of us all." But it does more than that. Just what does it create?

Conscience accomplishes very little, say some theologians. Notoriously unreliable, conscience must be fed the correct information from a higher source. It can be seared, mishandled, or misinformed until, like a compass thrown out of kilter by a proximate magnet, it gives an unreliable reading. Consequently, conscience is an interesting but indefinite and fickle function of personality.

It achieves too much, say many of the students of the psyche. Some psychologists claim that the conscience with archaic and perfectionistic standards makes the ego a prisoner within the confines of the individual's own personality, exercising a tyrannical reign, frequently escaped only by a leap into neurosis and psychosis. For these experts, conscience is a peculiar, primitive appurtenance of personality. It is comparable to the relationship of the appendix to the body and, like it, needs to be neutralized to prevent psychic disruption far more dangerous than a burst appendix and peritonitis.

A third view of conscience says it is the most wholesome and creative aspect of personality and helps men achieve their highest possibilities. This is the perspective of integrity therapy which views conscience as not only awesome in its power but persuasive in its influence, rewarding in its returns for cooperation, and exacting in its penalties for indifference. Conscience makes us into real persons, capable of reaching untold possibilities, says integrity therapy, as it demands a reexamination of the past loose thinking about this maligned function of personality.

It is a commentary on our highly developed technological era and our preoccupation with the machine, that we have so much difficulty in understanding an age-old mechanism of human personality. Nevertheless, this very machine age provides some of the best illustrations of a functioning conscience. Complex machinery requires sensitive mechanisms to warn against malfunctioning. There is a strange paradox in the sight of a man glued to the TV set while watching the countdown to a space shot. He hangs onto every message from the technicians hovered over their fluctuating gauges, flashing lights, purring buzzers, or clanging alarms. All the time he is unaware of his own personal intricate warning system. Periodically he guzzles liquor or gulps down tranquilizers in a vain effort to silence his conscience.

Unlike the rocket engineers, who with one indication from their gauges immediately shut off the power and search for the malfunction, man continues on his way to disaster. Master of the machines, he is unable to interpret the warning signals of his own personality. Busy at work, refining the warning systems of his mechanical monsters, he has neglected the study of the most complex and sensitive functioning of his own psychic makeup.

More akin to a custom-made instrument than a mass-produced measuring gauge, consciences come in assorted sizes, although the variety is not nearly as great as we sometimes imagine. Distinctly a human phenomenon, man is unique among the animals as he consciously, and sometimes unconsciously, looks over his life and behavior patterns, evaluating and passing judgment on them. His behavior is either in conformity with, or in conflict against, his value system. Conscience is the sensitive, flickering needle which measures the relationship of conduct and values.

The beachcomber constructs his abode with lumber chosen from the available offerings washed up by the waters of the seas. In somewhat the same manner a value system is built from a wide variety of raw materials gathered from the shores of life. Some values are carefully examined, chosen with deliberation, and rationally justified. Others are fashionable adaptations accepted on much the same ground as is an Easter bonnet and unthinkingly taken over from kith and kin, friends or groups of which we are members. Still others have upon them the impress of the Infinite.

The Rational Source

Despite accusations of superstition and taboo, evidence points to a rational source for many of man's values. The limitations and restrictions of moral standards which may seem so inconsistent and repressive to the impetuous youth are undergirded by pervasive logic so convincing that it has come to be accepted by the majority of people in any given society.

A college co-ed sought counseling. A girl of strong religious background, she was troubled by her recent episode of sexual misbehavior. She had a date with an attractive and much-sought-after male student and after a prolonged period of petting and a session in which he allayed her fears they had sexual relations. Returning to the campus in the automobile, the seducer was strangely silent. Finally he pulled over to the side of the highway and delivered a lecture to his friend on the dangers of promiscuity. His reasoning was very clear as he showed the possibilities of venereal disease, pregnancy, emotional involvement, loss of reputation, and the way in which promiscuity could jeopardize the prospects of marriage.

In what seems the height of contradiction the seducer, who in the heat of sexual desire could be very convincing, was now warning his victim of the dangers of the behavior he himself had led her into. This intelligent student realized morality was not irrational and unreasonable. There was a logical basis to it and in his calmer and unemotional moments he was able to present a rationale for widely accepted moral standards.

Havighurst and Taba made a study of adolescent character and personality of youth in a midwestern town. After the completion of the study they came up with four objectives for Prairie City. Two of these are: *Develop a social environment which rewards good moral behavior in all kinds of boys and girls*, and *Encourage the intellectualization of values and moral experiences*. The investigators maintain, "Thinking about moral experience leads to the formation of moral principles."[1] Lasting values always have a long-range logic.

The Idealized Society

Values also arise from the consensus of the *society* within which we live. The wisdom and experiences of a group of people over the years have led to the acceptance of certain standards of right and wrong. There has come the gradual realization that weaker members of society have to be protected and that certain types of behavior will damage the fabric of a community.

John Dewey, who has often been quoted to justify free and permissive attitudes, gives us an excellent exposition of the part that society plays in the formation of our values.

When a child acts, those about him react. They shower encouragement upon him, visit him with approval, or they bestow frowns and rebukes. What others do to us when we act is as natural a consequence of our action as what the fire does to us when we plunge our hands in it . . . In language and imagination we rehearse the responses of others just as we dramatically enact other consequences. We pass on the action. We know with them; there is conscience. An assembly is formed within our breast which discusses and appraises proposed and performed acts. The community without becomes a forum and tribunal within, a judgment seat of charges, assessments and exculpations. Our thoughts of our own actions are saturated with the ideas that others entertain about them, ideas which have been expressed not only in explicit instructions but still more effectively in reaction to our acts.[2]

The functioning of the social influences of others plays its considerable role in a growing value system.

Amid all the talk about relationship ethics it becomes even more important to explore the full implication of what relationship really is. The relationship basis of morality has been formulated by Kirkendall in one of his recent books. His distinction between morality and immorality is to be found in the way in which any behavior affects others. He states it like this:

Whenever a decision or a choice is to be made concerning behavior, the moral decision will be the one which works toward the creation of trust, confidence, and integrity in relationships. It should increase the capacity of individuals to cooperate, and enhance the sense of self-respect in the individual. Acts which create distrust, suspicion, and misunderstanding, which build barriers and destroy integrity, are immoral. They decrease the individual's sense of self-respect, and rather than producing a capacity to work together they separate people and break down the capacity for communication.[3]

There are two other considerations in Kirkendall's formula:

First, the dissolution of barriers needs to extend beyond the two-person association, or a tightly-knit small unit. This is to say that a good relationship leads its members toward an increasing acceptance of others, and others to an increasing acceptance of them. A good relationship between two or a few persons is like a stone cast in a pool of water. It creates an ever-widening circle of ripples which eventually reaches the farthest bank. This capacity to extend to and receive acceptance from an ever-expanding world is basic both to the mental health of individuals and to the stability and preservation of a society.

Second, consideration needs to be extended to long-range consequences. Certain experiences may create a closer relationship between two or more persons at a particular time, but how will it work out eventually? This is an important consideration.

Clear-cut, unequivocal answers to the questions posed by these two conditions will be impossible in many situations. Yet it is important to establish integrity and develop interpersonal relationships based upon trust, cooperation and goodwill, which, over the long run, will include more and more persons within their range.[4]

I once worked with a group of drug addicts in a hospital where they were serving periods of detention. At the beginning I was warned to be particularly careful about using the word "society." Most of them felt society had been very unjust in its dealings with them. Later, as we had discussions on morality and just what was right or wrong, I invited each of the addicts to give his definition of morality. Strangely enough almost every one of them made some mention of society. To define morality without alluding to society is virtually impossible.

The word "conscience" comes from the Latin *conscientia,* a word meaning "joint knowledge" or "the knowledge which we share with others." The Greek equivalent, *suneidasis,* also means joint knowledge, coming later to connote the knowledge of right and wrong. In each instance it related back to the group and society as a primary consideration in reaching values. This is not necessarily an endorsement of the faults and shortcomings of some societies. It is an *idealized* society which builds up and strengthens our best values.

The Voice of Transcendence

The third source of values, and for the believer the most important of all, is the revelation of deity. The socializing process moves out in ever-widening circles from the individual to others and on to larger groupings. But the expanding process does not conclude with even the mostly highly regarded groups in society. Religion is an attempt of the human to "raise his loyalties and value judgments to the level of the cosmic."[5] God is the name which symbolizes the highest in life and the concept of God is "the symbol of the collective at its best."[6]

A young woman in group therapy spoke about her despondency and efforts to find out what was wrong. She then added, "I went down through the Ten Commandments and tried to judge myself by them." Although not a particularly religious person, she was following a time-honored practice of troubled people.

In the Eastern Orthodox Church the penitent is instructed to prepare himself for confession by examining his conscience. This is done by reviewing the Ten Commandments and judging his life by them. Martin Luther's smaller catechism gives instructions to the penitent to confess his sins, and if he asks how he knows these, he is instructed: "Reflect on your condition in the light of the Ten Commandments." Paul said: "If it had not been for the law, I should not have known sin. I should not have known what it is to covet if the law had not said, "You shalt not covet."[8]

For many Christians the Ten Commandments and other specific moral teachings of the Bible are of greater importance than the opinions of a society or a subgroup. For them, as Frankl said, "Conscience is the voice of transcendence, man accepts the voice but does not originate it."[8] After contending that the sources of values are science, experience, and religion, Coleman[9] proceeds to the conclusion that man has traditionally looked to a revelation from God as the ultimate source of values.

Must and Ought

The evolution of a mature conscience is one of the wonders of the human psyche. Not unlike the confined chrysalis blossoming into fragile butterfly beauty, conscience ultimately so sensitive, passes through a long process of growth. It begins with rigid and sometimes seemingly unreasonable *do's* and *don't's*. In the dawning self-awareness, as early as the eighteenth month, a baby becomes vaguely aware of the restraints within his circumscribed society. Parents' restrictions of "no," "don't touch that," or, "you cannot go there," sometimes accompanied by punishment, bring painful recognition of the boundaries of life.

But even as the no's are accepted there comes the evolution of "you must." Following the negatives come the imperatives: You must wash your face, comb your hair; tidy your room; eat your breakfast; come when you are called; go to school.

Like the traveler rounding the bend to see the rolling valley in all its breathtaking and beckoning beauty is the ever-expanding world of the growing child. New horizons and vistas of attractive and inviting experiences beckon. But there are also the restrictive "no trespassing" areas and pathways which must be trodden, even though they are inconvenient and time-consuming. The boundaries and footpaths come to be respected, not just because of thundering voices from without, but because within is an insistent whisper as the voice of authority is internalized. By about the sixth year the "must" conscience has taken control.

The adolescent surge of sexuality, turmoil, and revolt frequently brings at least temporary rejection of parental authority, in varying degrees, and with it the growth of an "ought" conscience. Society's hedgings and restraints are no longer obeyed for fear of parental punishment but from a sense of obligation. The "musts" of life still remain but with widening experiences the "oughts" become more potent.

However, despite "the power of positive thinking," the so-called negative aspects, the "thou shalt not" of conscience, must never be underestimated. Running through the heart of fashionable Palm Beach, Florida, is a beautiful road which can easily be mistaken for highway A1A. At the entrance is a large sign: "This is *not* A1A." My guide remarked: "That's the first road sign I've ever seen telling what a road is not." Yet this negative sign serves an important purpose.

Conscience fulfils a useful function in its "Thou shalt not" as well as its "You ought" functionings. Only a minority of troubled people are in difficulty because they "left undone the things they ought to have done." Far more frequently the haunting specter is of bad choices and inappropriate, unrealistic, or antisocial behavior. The flickering needle of conscience is more specific and definite when the destructive danger point is neared.

The Language of Conscience

Conscience is sometimes described as the still small voice that tells us when we've done something wrong. But it is obviously far more complex than this. Its sensitivity and effectiveness has a time sequence related to the overt act. Before the experience the voice of conscience is specific and clear, as in unemotional and reasonable tones it either warns against or encourages toward the contemplated activity. Conscience' weakest moment probably comes immediately before or during the course of the act as desire, passion, or preoccupation drowns out its voice. It may remain until after the event for conscience to speak in its most strident tones. Like a modern computer with its remarkable ability to "store up" information available for reproduction upon a given signal, so conscience has tremendous capacity for recall. Unlike the computer, however, there is no convenient mechanical control to shut it off and cause it to cease producing the unhappy history of the past.

Because we fail to listen to the still small voice of conscience it has to speak in other ways. Like the skilful public relations man, using a diversity of media and techniques to get his message across, conscience has an infinite variety of communications techniques and methods of expression, sometimes so subtle it is almost impossible to interpret its pronouncements. Many of the reactions which throw us into such confusion are symptoms, called by Belgum "the amplified and distorted voice of conscience."[10]

Just as the secret dispatches are transmitted in code and must be deciphered before the communication can be understood, the coded message of conscience requires unscrambling before it can be made clear.

Boisen, in so many ways ahead of his time, was equally perceptive in discussing symptoms: "We must look back of the outward symptoms to the inner meaning of the experience in terms of the patient's own picture of himself and his own scale of values. What do the symptoms mean as regards the inner forces and motivations which make either for life or for death, for renewal or for destruction?"[11] Or, as Adolph Meyer states it, it is the function of the therapist to discover *the sense* in *the nonsense.* An examination of the language of conscience will be a first step toward the elucidation of the real meaning or meanings of any given symptom.

In *organ language* conscience expresses itself through the functioning of the body to bring suffering and discomfort. The so-called "functional" illnesses have no physical basis but bring about 50 percent of the patients to a doctor's office. Suffering from headache, stomach upset, heart palpitation, or any of a multitude of disorders, the functional illness is just as real as if the organ itself were damaged or diseased, yet, it comes from an entirely different source.

It was Gordon Allport who claimed that writers of literature might provide us with better insights into the functioning of personality than the highly trained psychological investigators. This provocative thought might be extended to the singers of folk songs. One popular group sang "The Unfortunate Miss Bailey."

A Captain bold in Halifax,
  Who dwelt in country quarters
Seduced a maid who hanged herself
  One Monday in her garters

His wicked conscience smited him,
  He lost his stomach daily.
He took up drinking ra-ta-fi—a
  And thought upon Miss Bailey.[12]

Conscience was at work in both Miss Bailey and the Captain of Halifax. She lost her life and he his stomach. His conscience was using organ language, a voice which he tried to drown in alcohol.

The word "conversion" does not have a religious connotation for the psychologist but refers to the converting of a mental conflict to a physical manifestation. Bushels of pills are taken, gallons of medicine quaffed down, and vast sums of money expended in an effort to gain relief by ineffectually trying to remove a symptom rather than listening to what may in reality be the voice of conscience.

Sometimes conscience expresses itself in *affective language*. The subject just doesn't "feel well." In the throes of depression, listlessness, anxiety, and fear, life feels hopeless and hardly worth the struggle. One counselee described it, "I don't know what triggers a period of depression. It's like a thick, black fog rolling in from nowhere." But it did in actual fact have a logical point of origin.

There is a tacit acknowledgment of the relationship of emotions and conscience in the frequently used expression "guilt feelings." Integrity therapy practitioners are quick to point out it is not "guilt feelings" but guilt, pure and simple, which is causing the trouble. The attendant gloom is one of the many

ways guilt is communicated. Nevertheless, depression is probably
the most frequently encountered indication of an offended conscience.

Thought language is seen in weird and unreal thought patterns
which make the sufferer feel different from all other people. A
counselee, composed and relaxed, told a remarkable story. The
children in her family constantly were being taken from her by
FBI agents, who replaced them with children looking exactly
like her own.

The group was astonished at the content of her delusion and
showed their skepticism by bombarding her with questions. To
these she responded with a quiet, knowing smile, which in effect
said, "I realize you can't really understand my experiences."

Later therapy revealed she had unsuccessfully tried to terminate her pregnancies. Although ineffectual, the attempts had left
their mark. The children she had once tried to be rid of were
now being taken away from her. (Thought processes were the
vehicle of her conscience.) ? No!!

Conscience may use *sensate language* in which the sensory
processes are thrown out of gear. A woman was bothered with
the sound of cars racing to the front of her house, then screeching
to a halt. No one else in the family could hear the nonexistent
automobiles. Later therapy revealed she was involved in an adul-
terous relationship and that her guilt now expressed itself through
distorted sensory processes.

Her conscience knew she deserved to have someone come after
her and provided her the experience through her senses.

"Voices" and other hallucinations indicate a stirring of the
deeper levels of the mental life, something which in itself may
be helpful as well as destructive. Their chief significance lies in
what they may reveal as to the inner trends and attitudes. What
the voices say is always the important question, not the mere fact
of hearing voices.[18]

The compulsive reactions in which the sufferer must perform certain "meaningless acts," such as washing one's hands, may themselves be *action language*, and not nearly as meaningless as has sometimes been imagined. Shakespeare's portrayal of Lady Macbeth shows the connection between the murder of Banquo and the compulsive handwashing. Rather than being "meaningless," the compulsive activity makes good sense when seen as a manifestation of conscience.

Counselors speak of nonverbal language to describe the expressive actions of troubled people. Conscience has its *language of behavior*. Deviant conduct is often carried on at such an obvious level that it demands attention. A prominent lay worker in a church was confronted with the evidence of his homosexual activities which had been practiced in a very open manner. His response was, "Thank goodness, you caught me at last."

The notorious slaying of thirty-year-old Frances Brown in Chicago some years ago had the most bizarre associations but none more remarkable than the words on the beige living room wall. In red lipstick, with letters ranging from four to six inches high, it read: "For heavens sake catch me before I kill more. I cannot control myself."[14]

Handsome, seventeen-year-old William Heirers, the writer of the message, committed three murders and hundreds of burglaries in the Chicago area. Heirer's message has been described as a "cry for help," which was obvious. But it would be more accurate to describe it as a cry of conscience.

Dream language offers a vehicle for the expression of conscience. An infamous "madam" in her biography tells the story of getting started in her "business." She reasoned that running a house of prostitution would be an easy way to live, and was soon established in a comfortable apartment, with a self-confident glow of success. But when she went to sleep at night she had a recurring dream of her father's chasing her down the street and shouting: "Whore, bum!" Dreams sometimes referred to as "the royal road to the unconscious" may more correctly be "the royal road to the conscience."

All of us know of a particular type of insensitive person who joins in group activities, makes outrageous statements, and continues on, blissfully unaware of his listeners' antagonistic reactions. We say of him, "He just doesn't get the message." The voice of conscience is sometimes loud and clear but, unfortunately, *we* don't get the message. Failing to interpret just what conscience is saying, we go through needless suffering and distress.

Conscience, Friend or Foe?

One convenient way of accounting for the forces and conflicts within personality is to think of systems involving checks and balances. The id is the primitive force, the ego the decision-making self, and the superego, or "greater I," the conscience. Freud claimed the superego, or conscience, was constantly urging the ego to strive for an unrealistic perfection, thus keeping the individual in misery. Some of the suggestions used by Freudians in their therapeutic work include:

Modify inappropriate superego controls so that the patient can with less conflict and anxiety . . . successfully pursue erotic goals.[15]
The superego is modified and its severity reduced.[16]
Liberate the individual as completely as possible from anachronistic values, attitudes strivings and defenses.[17]

These clearly indicate the Freudian bias against conscience.

Boisen faced this problem in his personal life. Bothered with a sexual problem, while hospitalized with his psychotic episode he tried to talk with the doctor about his case. He describes his experience:

That particular hospital took the organicist point of view. The doctors did not believe in talking with the patients about their symptoms, which they assumed to be rooted in some yet undiscovered organic difficulty. The longest time I ever got was fifteen minutes, during which the very charming young doctor *pointed out that one must not hold the reins too tightly in dealing with the sex instinct. Nature he said must have its way.*[18]

In his refusal to accept the organicistic or amoral theorizing, Boisen was led to an entirely different perspective. Looking back over life's experience, in his autobiography he says: "The present day tendency to seek the solution of a troublesome sex drive by lowering the conscience threshold and looking upon sex as a natural desire to be lightly satisfied is something which seems to me to be a serious mistake." He came to conclude that mental illness was really a disorganization of the patient's world. An epic credo offered by Boisen to the Twenty-fifth Anniversary Conference of the Council for Clinical Pastoral Training in 1950 summarized his convictions.

I believe that the real evil in functional mental illness is not to be found in discontent with one's imperfections, even when that discontent is carried to the point of severe disturbance, but in the sense of estrangement and isolation due to the presence of instinctual claims which can neither be controlled nor acknowledged for fear of condemnation. The aim of psychotherapy is not to get rid of the conflict by lowering the conscience threshold, but to remove the sense of alienation by restoring the sufferer to the (internalized fellowship of the best) and thus setting him free to strive for his true objectives in life.[19]

Boisen would have no part nor lot in downgrading the role of conscience in individual development.

Mowrer, after many years of following Freud, is altogether opposed to this psychoanalytic concept. He sets out his alternative idea in the following diagrams.

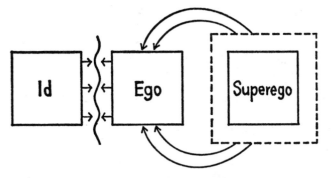

Fig. 1. Schematic representation of the "dynamics" of neurosis, as conceived by Freud. A "hypertrophied" superego, or conscience, supposedly lays siege to the ego and takes it captive. Then the superego forces the ego to reject the claims of the id for any expression or satisfaction of its "instinctual demands." The result is that a sort of "iron curtain" is constructed between ego and id (see wavy line); and dissociation or "repression" is said to be in force. Neurosis proper ("anxiety") consists of the "unconscious danger" that the force of the id will succeed in breaking through this "wall" and overwhelming the ego; and a constant, devitalizing expenditure of energy by the ego is necessary to keep up its "defenses."[30]

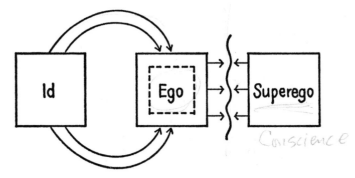

Fig. 2. A modified interpretation of the state called neurosis. Here it is assumed that the ego is taken captive, not by the superego, but by the id, and that it is now the "voice of conscience" that is rejected and dissociated. "Anxiety" thus arises, not because of a threatened return of repressed energies of the id, but because of the unheeded railings and anger of conscience. Here it is not assumed that there is any difference in the "size" or strength of these three aspects of personality, unless it is that the ego is somewhat weak and undeveloped.[21]

Mowrer states his position:

In essence Freudian theory holds that anxiety comes from evil wishes, from acts which the individual would commit if he dared. The alternative view here proposed is that anxiety comes, not from acts which the individual would commit but dares not, but from acts which he *has committed*, but wishes that he had not. It is, in other words, a "guilt theory" of anxiety rather than an "impulse theory."[22]

There is nothing more disconcerting than to be driving down the highway and suddenly see a red light flashing on the instrument panel. There are two ways of responding to the situation. The most ridiculous of all would be to attack the gauge and destroy it so it would not respond to the oil level in the motor. Yet, this is exactly what the protesters against the positive role of conscience are suggesting. Erikson's comment is particularly relevant: "We must grudgingly admit that even as we were trying to devise, with scientific determinism, a therapy for the few, we were led to promote an ethical disease among the many."[23]

Common sense indicates the most appropriate response to a warning light would be to stop, check, remedy the defect, and confidently continue the journey. Conscience is at the same time the sign of both our weaknesses and our finer sensitivities. The word Epictetus penned in the first century A.D., speaks just as clearly as when it was written:

When we were children our parents handed us over to a nursery slave who should watch over us everywhere lest harm befall us. But when we were grown up, God hands us over to the conscience implanted in us, to protect us. Let us not in any way despise its protection for should we do so we shall be both ill-pleasing to God and have our own conscience as an enemy.

3

THE GOODNESS OF GUILT

"At my request, the jury then was polled individually, and twelve more times the word 'guilty' filled the courtroom. It was like an echo: guilty, guilty, guilty."[1]

As familiar as we are with Perry Mason, who-dunits, and courtroom dramas, we have come to believe that the ultimate in human experience is to be declared "not guilty." But even in legal circles there has been endless debate as to when the defendant can be held responsible for his actions and fairly adjudged legally guilty. English law has a provision for "diminished responsibility," when the offender is said to be mentally unbalanced at the time of the act. Psychiatrists are called upon to present evidence to show the defendant's emotional disturbance. If this can be established he may be held not responsible for his action, and acquitted.

Now has come a turn in the tide. Even psychiatrists and psychologists have convinced the jurists that the mentally ill person should not be held responsible for his actions. Some of them are reconsidering the whole area of responsibilty and the part it plays in mental illness. One theory now being widely propagated in the circles of psychotherapy is that the emotionally disturbed person should not only be held responsible for his actions, but that his very condition has been brought on by irresponsibility.

Among these new voices are heard men like Szass, Mowrer, and Glasser. Glasser states the situation:

Responsibility, a concept basic to Reality Therapy, is here de-fined as the ability to fulfill one's needs, and to do so in a way that does not deprive others of the ability to fulfill their needs. . . . A responsible person also does that which gives him a feeling of self-worth and a feeling that he is worthwhile to others. . . .

Acquiring responsibility is a complicated lifelong problem. *Although we are given unchanging needs from birth to death, needs which, if left unsatisfied, cause us or others to suffer, we are not naturally endowed with the ability to fulfill them.* If the ability to fulfill our needs were as much a part of man as are the needs themselves, there would be no psychiatric problems. This ability must, however, be learned. . . . *Our concern is with those who have not learned, or* who have lost the ability—those who fill our mental hospitals and prisons, our psychiatric clinics and offices.

Throughout the remainder of this book *these people are de-scribed as irresponsible.*[2]

If Glasser's reasoning is correct, the whole concept of "dimin-ished responsibility" may involve a strange anomaly. An indi-vidual who drifts through life without accepting the normal ob-ligations of human experience may become "mentally ill." This condition in turn absolves him from liability for the outcome of his own actions and sets up a vicious cycle with the last state worse than the first for both the individual and his society. The alternative view is that a big part of the price of human existence is the process of becoming accountable. Coleman says the path-way of maturity is from "irresponsibility to responsibility." A growth of responsibility inevitably gives rise to the experience called "guilt."

The common notion of guilt is of an unrelenting and tyranni-cal force, creating misery and unhappiness for man. But this is only part of its role. There is a sense in which "all upbringing is a cultivation of a sense of guilt on an intensive scale."[3] The child gradually learns the limits of life which, along with apprehended imperatives, are internalized and later triggered into behavior by the stimulus called guilt. It has been said that "a capacity to experience guilt-feelings is a necessary attribute of the healthy person . . . part of the price we pay for the privilege of being human (moral) beings."[4] That this awesome power within the human personality gives meaning to human experiences was indicated by Tournier when he said that "a guilty conscience is the seasoning of our daily life."[5]

As important as the sense of guilt might be to the individual, it pales into insignificance when compared with its role in society. Some anthropologists divide cultures into two groups, guilt cultures and shame cultures. A *shame culture* is that within which social control is achieved by the ridicule or criticism of others. The wrongness may not be so much in the deed as it is in being found out. A *guilt culture*, on the other hand, relies on the individual conscience as a means of social control. People who have lived for any time in one of the so-called "shame cultures" heave a sigh of relief when they return again to a guilt culture which rests upon the basis of the citizen's responsibility to society's rules.

The social aspects of guilt provide the basis for an unusual article by Mowrer on the subject of "Why I Don't Drink."[6] Alcohol is sometimes called a "superego solvent," because of the way in which it dulls the finer sensitivities and allows the imbiber to participate in behavior not normally practiced. To the claim that drinking increases an individual's sociability, Mowrer counters that it involves a singular contradiction. If conscience is "the internalized voice of society," anything that anesthetizes it—puts the drinker out of touch with society and its requirements of him—is actually antisocial. The really social man is the one who is aware of his obligations to society and in a condition of uneasiness when these obligations are ignored or transgressed.

Without a sense of guilt a western society deteriorates. Goodhart says, "The strength of English law, from the basic rules of

the constitution to the minor regulations issued by legal authority, depends in large part on the fact that the people of this
country recognize that they are under an obligation to obey the
law."[7] In any well ordered society, sociopaths, with their low
level of guilt, are so destructive that they have to be placed in a
penitentiary or a mental hospital, hopefully to reform them, but
generally, more realistically, to save the community from their
incursions.

Keeping It Under Your Hat

A Word War II story tells of a Jewish couple living under the
Nazi regime in Germany. Anticipating their arrest and incarceration in a concentration camp, they made plans for the care of
their paralyzed son. An agreement was reached with a one-legged
veteran who, in return for caring for the boy, was to receive the
lease of their apartment. The couple's arrest followed, whereupon the veteran smuggled the boy away to a mountain cabin,
where he was left with a meager supply of food and certain
death.

The veteran rationalized that he had fulfilled his agreement
and sold the apartment lease to acquire his ill-gotten gains. A
strange experience followed. One morning he noticed a lump
about the size of a pigeon's egg on his forehead. He pressed the
bump which disappeared only to pop out at the back of his
skull. Giving it another push it showed up over his ear. Pressured from this spot it came out again on the top of his head. He
felt this was a distinctive improvement, for he could now cover
it with his hat.

In his parable the author has depicted a typical human reaction
wherein an individual's guilt, apparently successfully concealed,
"pops up" in a most unexpected way. Although it may be dis-
guised by apt dissembling, it has a disconcerting habit of suddenly appearing. Even though it may be kept "under one's hat,"

he always lives in anticipation of someone's sidling up and whispering, "Your guilt is showing."

James R. Donovan's story of the Russian spy, Colonel I. Abel, tells of a scene in court, while Abel was waiting out the process of trial.

All of his life had been filled with waiting—some of it so pointless. He had waited to keep secret meetings, waited to pick up a message at a drop, waited for the right moment to recruit an agent, waited for letters from his family, and waited and feared for the moment when he might be found out. Abel sometimes felt as though everyone he passed on the street was looking at him and knew who he was. He once told me he had enjoyed reading the autobiography of bank robber Willie Sutton, a celebrated fugitive who had suffered nightmares in which hundreds of people pointed at him and screamed, "You're Willie Sutton." Abel explained that any undercover fugitive must constantly fight against the feeling that the whole world is on the verge of guessing his secret.[8]

Although it was for him a matter of life and death, Abel's reactions are typical of anyone who has lived a "closed life." It does not have to be international espionage. In many of the everyday experiences of life the subject keeps certain events carefully concealed. As a consequence, he lives in a state of anxiety lest his well-kept secret should leak out and become known. He is forever waiting.

"Guilt feelings," probably the most widely used expression concerning guilt, can be misleading. It really refers to only one particular manifestation of the subjective experience. Guilt is really a condition which arises from the contravention of a conceived value system which may be expressed through feelings or a variety of reactions. Any effort to confine guilt to "feelings" follows a common misapprehension which ignores the infinite variety of ways in which guilt may manifest itself.

Psychoeconomics

The word guilt has a significant root. Originally it was the payment of a fine for an offense. It comes to us from the Anglo-Saxon word "gylt," meaning "to pay." At a conference on integrity therapy, a rabbi pointed out that in Yiddish the word "gelt" means "money." Of guilt, Tournier says: "It is inscribed on the human heart: everything must be paid for."[9] McKenzie asserts: "Guilt must be paid for."[10]

Many models have been chosen to represent the operations of the mind but a consideration of the root meaning of guilt suggests that any discussion of this factor in personality could more logically center upon a consideration of psychoeconomics. One woman's symptom took the form of lavish spending, and troubled people will frequently say, "When I feel bad I just go out and buy something." But many guilt payments are far more subtle than this and may take any number of forms.

Payments of guilt are often unwittingly made. While it is widely accepted that the unregulated urges operate at the unconscious level, the fact that the superego or conscience may also function below the level of awareness is frequently overlooked. Yet even some psychoanalysts have noted the unconscious activity of the superego. Unconscious guilt is generally overlooked and consequently its symptoms are misinterpreted.

Perhaps, in part, because I was a child of the great trade depression I am careful with my money. Some who know me might be unkind enough to use the word "chinchy." It will probably surprise my critics to learn that I regularly gave away sums of money over a period of years. The cashier of our "institution" called to inquire about my son, long since married and now with a daughter of his own. Under our health insurance, salary deductions had been made for his medical coverage, although his marriage had disqualified him from benefits. I immediately claimed a refund, but the company declined to return the money paid. My inward consternation can easily be imagined. For years I had paid out my money, blissfully ignorant of my unwitting generosity. I just didn't realize the payments were being made.

Unconscious guilt is a constant paying process. Like the careless businessman whose assets are being dissipated we may be altogether unaware of the cost of unresolved guilt. This is another reason why guilt *feelings* are not really as important as it is popularly maintained. We can be subjects of an unperceived guilt which, like the sly desert predators, will come creeping out when least expected and show itself in a multitude of ways, bearing little resemblance to the original causative factors.

Unconscious guilt sometimes reveals itself in defensive aggression. If a wife feels aggressive toward her husband and annoyed and provoked by trivialities of his behavior, a good question for her to ask is, "In what way have I done something wrong toward him?" If she is honest and thinks a while she will generally find an answer. This type of guilt reaction is frequently seen in adolescence. The concerned parent sits down to try to discuss suspicious behavior, only to be greeted with an aggressive outburst. Ostensibly a show of righteous indignation at such an unfair accusation, in reality this may be nothing more than an elaborate smoke screen to cover guilt.

Another unconscious guilt reaction is to blame someone else. In the story of Adam and Eve, Adam's response to the question as to why he had eaten from the forbidden tree was to blame Eve. Eve in turn passed the blame on to the serpent. The mental mechanism of rationalization has been called "the counterfeit of reason." It is possible to develop an elaborate reasoning process to steer attention away from one's own deficiencies and to place behavioral responsibility on a convenient scapegoat.

Payment of guilt may take the form of projecting it onto other people. Under great stress, Mr. Smithers came to tell the counselor of his wife's unfaithfulness. She was having sex relations with other men. He had never actually caught her, but he could see by her crinkled dress, use of the car, and dozens of other little things that she was misbehaving with other males. The past middle-aged wife was in turn astounded, hurt, and frustrated as she faced these charges and produced clear and incontrovertible evidence to prove her innocence. But it was all to no avail, nothing could convince her husband. As therapy proceeded, it became obvious that the man himself had misbehaved sexually. Payment for his own misdeeds took the form of seeing his wife perform the very acts of which he himself was guilty, and so inflicting on him his well-deserved punishment.

Unfaced guilt is the great blackmailer. The victim hides his failures by putting on a brave face to the world. But he is pressured in myriad ways to make the payments to guarantee that his secret will not be revealed. The psychic resources of the victim are being constantly depleted and the best aspects of the human experience are extorted from him. No matter how great his material wealth, he lives in psychic squalor and poverty.

The "Overguilty" Person

In any discussion concerning the role of guilt in human experience one question is asked with monotonous regularity, "What of the person who is just too guilty and worries over multitudinous small, unimportant things? Is this guilt healthy? Shouldn't something be done to reduce this destructive force?

Scrupulosity is the word generally used to describe a person who is obsessed with petty and unimportant matters and who is frequently overwhelmed by feelings of unworthiness. Often seen in religious circles, scrupulous individuals are pointed to as examples of one of the most unfortunate aspects of religious experience and the false guilt it engenders.

Mrs. Wilson, a widow struggling to support a family of three children, comes seeking counsel from her minister. She is worried and anxious. With only a meager income, she feels her contributions to the church are far too small. But it is impossible for her to do any better, and as a result she remains in a state of turmoil.

The pastor points out the smallness of her income and shows that on a percentage basis her giving more than favorably compares with that of others. He finally convinces her there is really no reason why she should feel this way, and apparently the problem is solved.

Next week sees Mrs. Wilson back in the church office again. With the shamefaced appearance of a criminal caught in the act, she tells of the awful event of last Sunday when her ten-year-old daughter picked some flowers from the planter in the front of the church. The minister smiles kindly, commends her honesty, and recalls the fruit he stole in boyhood days. He notes it did not make him an habitual criminal. After a prayer to God on her behalf, Mrs. Wilson, wearing a seraphic smile, is dismissed.

Just ten days later she returns to tell how disturbed she is that her work takes so much time that she cannot accept the invitation of the nominating committee to teach a Sunday School class. Since refusing, she has been unable to sleep and is in a constant state of anxiety. Once more the pastor takes time to help her see that there is no real basis for her concern and thus brings relief to her troubled spirit.

But it is only temporary. Mrs. Wilson continues to make her periodic appearances in the minister's office to tell of her lack of faith, improper beliefs, or slackness in religious service. The minister is finally reduced to avoiding his troubled parishioner.

On the surface, Mrs. Wilson is a sensitive soul whose standards are so high she will remain forever guilty. The only apparent way out of the dilemma is to work at reducing Mrs. Wilson's guilt so that she can live a normal life.

But a closer look at Mrs. Wilson may show another aspect of her experience. Apparently the very model and example of a desire to do right, she may be using an elaborate defense to cover up her real guilt. A critical look at other areas of her life will probably show there is something really big about which Mrs. Wilson is guilty, and all her anxiety about the minutiae of her life is really an exaggerated concealment device.

A student came by my office to talk. I had encountered him in the library where he was calling the attention of a staff member to a damaged book and speaking of the irresponsibility of students who mutilate materials. Noting my arrival, he asked if he could have a conference and an appointment was made. Sitting in my office he said he wanted to be open with me and tell me that during the last semester he had reported reading a book in my course, but now wished to confess he had not really read it but only skimmed through it.

I encouraged him to continue talking. Then I shared an experience of failure in my own life. Following a brief silence came a story of serious personal irresponsibility. Concern about the mutilated library book and a misreported reading was an elaborate evasion. Behind the facade of concern for other matters lay his real guilt.

In both of these cases, like a bird feigning a broken wing to lure the intruder from her nestlings, the subjects are saying, "Look what a good person I am, worried about all these little things."

This apparent piety and concern may be the most blatant fakery and subterfuge of all.

Any attempt to help Mrs. Wilson or the student by the reduction of apparent guilt will simply delay the process of discovering *real* guilt. Also delayed will be finally putting the sufferer's feet on the pathway to openness, activity, and an adequate adjustment to life.

The Constructive Use of Guilt

Psychotherapy is obviously a discipline much concerned with guilt. As we noted in an earlier chapter, a lot of therapeutic work has aimed at the reduction of guilt. But in the new emphasis, the constructive role of this powerful force is being highlighted by Dr. Glasser in his work with delinquent girls in the Ventura school. He tells of a particularly difficult case:

All during therapy and especially toward the time that she would ordinarily have been considered ready for parole, I pointed out to her that she had little feeling for anyone in the world except herself. I told her that as much as I enjoyed talking to her and as well as she seemed to be doing at times in the kitchen program, unless she began to consider the rights and feelings of other people, both here at the school and in the community, she would go right back to being a thief when she left. I always emphasized the word *thief*, never glossing over the offense with milder euphemism, shoplifter. At the same time I heard that in the cottage she did everything possible to avoid work while still looking as if she was busy.[11]

Glasser's emphasis indicates his view of the constructive role of guilt. She would continue to put on an act, living life irresponsibly and damaging to herself and the community, unless she developed a healthy and necessary awareness of guilt.

As therapy progressed the girl continued to misbehave and Glasser had her sent to the discipline cottage. This had a discernible effect on her.

She was greatly changed. She asked me how long she would have to stay in the discipline cottage. Saying that I would leave it up to her to tell me when she was ready to leave, I helped her by adding that she could prepare for leaving by telling the truth and changing some of her ways. She then poured out the story of her deceitful life, her lies and misbehavior at the school, and how worried she was about her future. Instead of forgiving her, which used to be my natural impulse, before I discovered how wrong it is therapeutically, I told her she was right to feel miserable and probably would continue to feel bad for the next few weeks. When I left I told her I would see her next week. Her desire to stay in discipline was therapeutic—knowing that she had thinking to do and feelings of guilt to overcome, she realized that the discipline cottage was the best place for her.

In Reality Therapy it is important not to minimize guilt when it is deserved, and Jeri deserved to feel as bad as she did.[12]

It is of particular note that Glasser doesn't just accept her in a "nonjudgmental" manner, which frequently means excusing behavior, but leaves her to "stew in her own juice." Through his attitude she realizes her own need to accept responsibility for her wrongdoing.

In a similar manner, integrity therapy provides a setting in which anxious people can become aware of their guilt. Critics of the theory are concerned that it is too "negative" and becomes unnecessarily harsh and cruel for a subject already bowing beneath life's pressures. In answer, it must be asserted that this is really the most positive of all therapeutic approaches. As the troubled person faces his symptoms and their underlying causes, the integrity therapist can say in all sincerity, "This suffering of yours is not an indication of weakness, it is a sign of strength. It shows you have some character. If you had no real character structure you wouldn't be worried and upset. Your malaise is a barometer of your value system which will not allow you to continue to live at this lower level." Thus integrity therapy has a paradoxical emphasis of awareness, of failure and commendation, for the sensitivity which brought on the symptom. Such an attitude is the basis upon which true ego strength is built.

Although guilt is related to law, ethics, and psychotherapy, its closest association is with religion. It has an intimate relationship with the great doctrines of the Christian faith: atonement, reconciliation, justification by faith, and forgiveness of sin. Guilt is the raw subjective material out of which religious experience is forged. Dealing with, and accounting for, guilt engages the attention of the theologian. This also highlights the fallacy of religious voices raised in protest against any mention of guilt and insists on the necessity of a new permissive attitude which will vanquish the villainous monster guilt. Even as the religious person, like Samson of old, pulls down the pillars of guilt, he may be unwittingly demolishing the whole structure of religious experience, leaving only wreck, ruin, and desolation.

It is sometimes said that whereas psychoanalysis reduces guilt, integrity therapy builds it up. This is not right. It would be far closer to the truth to say that integrity therapy insists on facing the reality of guilt. It helps the individual realize just what his values really are and how he has been cheating himself. Guilt, like pain, is viewed as a healthy early warning signal which will help to save him from a course of self-defeating behavior.

If guilt is blackmail, it is also a goad. The victim who tires of extortion and finally tells his shameful story, often discovers that his new courage in admitting his transgression has created a new and unexpected climate for worthwhile living. Guilt can be the instrument for making the cowardly cringer into a new and meaningful person.

4

SOCIALIZATION: ITS PITFALLS AND POSSIBILITIES

Man is a social animal. Although other animals are gregarious and live in communities, none has such a highly developed experience of community and communication as does man. Any human not in some way involved in group life is looked upon as unusual, and if completely divorced from his fellows is considered abnormal. As was noted in the discussion of conscience, socialization plays an important role in building the individual's standards. In this sense it is a primary factor in the arousal of guilt, a process sometimes referred to as "oversocialization."

A group may exercise a strange influence on its members. There has been much theorizing as to just what the effects of the group on the individual are. The Frenchman Le Bon, in his early monumental work on *The Crowd* concluded that in the interaction and influence which the constituent group members had on each other, their individuality receded, and a "group mind" came into existence. This "group mind" had a ready response to an emotional appeal and a slow response to an intellectual one. So the "crowd" became an easy target for the demagogue and the rabble-rouser.

While few today would agree with this theorizing, there is obviously a pronounced effect of the group on its members. In the past we have spent much time focusing on the negative aspects of "the mob" or "the crowd," as seen in delinquent gangs and irresponsible and destructive mobs, and frequently overlooked the tremendous possibility for healing, support, and strengthening which comes from group life.

This positive role of the group was made clear from investigations carried out with American soldiers during World War II. It is frequently theorized that GI's were motivated by their patriotic ideals on the one hand and their hatred of the enemy on the other. Rather, this research indicated it was loyalty to a unit and relationships with the primary group. The primary group "served two principle functions in combat motivation: it *set and emphasized group standards* of behavior, and it *supported and sustained the individual* in stresses he would otherwise not be able to withstand."[1] The formal organization set the goals, but it was the primary groups from which the particular soldier drew his strength. One of the most significant efforts to account for the psychological aspects of the individual and his group has been made by Harry Stack Sullivan who, in his reaction against theories of personality based on biological concepts, emphasized the social basis of human experiences in his *Interpersonal Theory of Psychiatry*. He sees personality as "the relatively enduring pattern of recurrent interpersonal situations which characterized a human life."[2] Whereas in the past there has been endless discussion about the relationship of id, ego, and superego, and similar intrapsychic phenomena, Sullivan stresses the interpersonal situations, for the individual does not really exist apart from his relations with other people. Even a hermit lives with the memory of former personal relationships which continues to influence the way he thinks and acts. Only interpersonal reactions give real meaning to life.

In the functioning of group life it can be confidently predicted that groups may have an extraordinary influence on, and sometimes an unusual ministry of healing for, their members. An examination of four particularly influential groups should produce some principles of value in any form of group therapy.

The Early Church

Christianity itself began as a small group movement. Jesus obviously had a ministry to the multitudes who flocked to hear his words. But this wider ministry to the crowds was counterbalanced with a relationship to a smaller and more intimate group. As his ministry progressed, he spent more time with a smaller number of perceptive and responsive followers. Standards of discipleship were high and it sometimes seemed as if Jesus attracted by repelling, and only those willing to follow the path of self-denial could join the select band.

A special closeness existed within this group, with Jesus repeatedly withdrawing from a wider ministry to be with the more intimate inner circle. To them he confided his hopes and fears and they were left with the responsibility of propagating his teachings.

Following the day of Pentecost the infant church, a curious amalgam of heterogeneous religious and national elements, faced the threat of persecution from both religious and civil authorities. Like settlers in a new country, they drew closer together in an effort not only to stave off the attacks but to counterattack as "the terrible meek," by propagating their newly discovered faith.

Koinōnia, or fellowship, became the keynote of this apostolic group. From the statement that "they continued stedfastly in the apostles' doctrine and fellowship, and in breaking of bread, and in prayers" (Acts 2:42), it becomes obvious that fellowship, literally meaning going shares or having in common, was placed on a par with doctrine, the Lord's Supper, and prayer, specific worship and religious functions often separated from the fellowship experience in modern thinking.

Standards of church life were unusually high, with transgressors rebuked for failure to live up to the requirements of their religious profession. The sharing spirit was so strong that there even developed a community of goods in which they pooled all they owned and shared it with their fellow Christians. Though short-lived, the experiment was indicative of the kinship felt by individual members with each other.

Small groups were the order of the day in this early church. Owning no buildings, they gathered in homes as convenient meeting places, clustering together and continuing to make a rapid cell-like growth as groups grew and proliferated.

Lay leadership characterized the infant church. The leaders were fishermen, politicians, tax-gatherers and tentmakers. Few, if any of them, were graduates of the schools for training the ecclesiastical leaders of their day. The rapid growth of the early church was itself mute evidence of the effectiveness of the lay leadership.

This early church followed the practice of confession made to the whole group. The later development of a clerical leadership saw the practice still continued, with an insistence that even confession of sin in private should be followed by revealing it publicly to the church. Not until the third century was there a move toward private confession and this very frequently on the basis that public confession might cause scandal. Thus came the "sealing of the confessional."

Later consolidation of church life brought with it the growth of a hierarchy, construction of buildings and a burgeoning treasury, leading to material success and spiritual stagnation. The memory of the vitality of these early, vigorous, and highly successful days has rightfully haunted the church which is periodically visited with a revival of the group spirit.

The Methodist Class Meeting

The Methodist Church was originally a small group movement functioning within the Church of England. John Wesley, himself a priest of the Established Church, had a period of barren ministry in England and America. Finally, while meeting with some Moravian Christians, he had a "heartwarming" experience. The episode catapulted Wesley into a fervent evangelistic enterprise, destined to have a wide-reaching influence on the social and political life of England. The societies Wesley commenced were an adjunct to the regular Church of England services.

Two distinctives of this movement stand out. Laymen occupied a place of prominence. One of Wesley's converts wished to preach, and although Wesley's high church background led him to resist such a suggestion at first, he finally capitulated, and lay preachers and lay leaders played an important role in the new movement. As the Sunday School movement developed concomitantly with, and encouraged by, Methodism, it was characteristically a layman's movement. Often the clergy was indifferent and sometimes overtly hostile to the enterprise. Actually, in many instances, the enterprise lived a separate existence from the church.

A second and allied characteristic of Methodism was the development of a practical organization within which evolved the *class-meeting*.

Definite rules were promulgated and helped give rise to a number of distinctives.

1. The original groups were "seeking Christian perfection."
2. They met weekly.
3. No fewer than five, no more than ten gathered, with men, women, and unmarried persons in separate bands.
4. The leader commenced by telling his own state, sins, and temptations, then invited the rest of the group to tell their experiences.
5. All of this was done in the strictest of confidence.[3]

The place of laymen, high standards, openness of life, and constant meeting in small groups were the hallmarks of the powerful early days of the class meeting in Methodism.

The Oxford Group

This was another example of an organization emphasizing small groups, lay leadership, and confessional experiences. Frank Buckman, originally an ordained Lutheran minister, after a conversion experience became a personal evangelism lecturer at Hartford Seminary. He later left the seminary to engage in worldwide evangelism and was responsible for the formation of the Oxford Group Movement.

The Oxford Group was foremost of all a layman's movement of people, loosely knit together, highlighting the "changed life," as conversion was called. It emphasized a series of steps: Confidence, which came from speaking truthfully to another about one's life: confession—conviction—a sense of wrongdoing, guilt; conversion, acceptance of an altered way of life; and continuance, helping others as the person himself had been helped.

Sharing was an integral part of their procedure. At their meetings people were encouraged to make both public and private confessions. Confession was also used in the approach of members to outsiders. This was called "sharing for witness." It referred to the practice of telling someone else about sins committed in the past and now mastered. The idea was to establish rapport.

The central assumptions of the Oxford Group are:

1. Men are sinners.
2. Men can be changed.
3. Confession is a prerequisite to change.
4. The changed soul has direct access to God.
5. The age of miracles has returned (through changed lives, miraculous incidents, etc.).
6. Those who have been changed must change others.[4]

The group lived by high ethical standards and emphasized the four absolutes: *Honesty, purity, unselfishness,* and *love*. These absolutes became a target for many orthodox Christians who felt that the group was making a new effort to establish an impossible standard of Christian perfection.

Small groups, informality, lay leadership, high ethical standards, and the practice of confession were all characteristics of the Oxford Group.

Alcoholics Anonymous

Possibly the most dramatically successful of all these small group movements is itself a derivation of the Oxford Group and now widely known as Alcoholics Anonymous. The Oxford Group sponsored a mission for alcoholics at the Calvary Episcopal Church where Bill W., an alcoholic, became associated with them and achieved a degree of sobriety. Moving to Ohio and feeling the need of fellowship in his struggle, he got in touch with a surgeon, Dr. Bob, who also had been in contact with the Oxford Group. Soon the two men launched themselves on a campaign to help other alcoholics and so the movement grew and multiplied.

Possibly the best way of catching the spirit of Alcoholics Anonymous and what it means to individuals is to look at their Twelve Steps and Twelve Traditions.

We:
1. Admitted we were powerless over alcohol — that our lives had become unmanageable.
2. Came to believe that a Power greater than ourselves could restore us to sanity.
3. Made a decision to turn our will and our lives over to the care of God as we understood Him.
4. Made a searching and fearless moral inventory of ourselves.
5. Admitted to God, to ourselves, and to another human being the exact nature of our wrongs.
6. Were entirely ready to have God remove all these defects of character.

7. Humbly asked Him to remove our shortcomings.

8. Made a list of all persons we had harmed and became willing to make amends to them all.

9. Made direct amends to such people whenever possible, except when to do so would injure them or others.

10. Continued to take personal inventory and when we were wrong, promptly admitted it.

11. Sought through prayer and meditation to improve our conscious contact with God as we understood Him, praying only for knowledge of His will for us and the power to carry that out.

12. Having had a spiritual awakening as the result of these steps, we tried to carry this message to alcoholics and to practice these principles in all our affairs.[5]

It will be noted that there is a strong emphasis on the moral aspects of drinking, an acknowledgment of shortcoming, a change of life, and a new missionary zeal. The basis of group life is to be found in the Twelve Traditions, which are:

1. Our common welfare should come first; personal recovery depends upon A.A. unity.

2. For our group purpose there is but one ultimate authority —a loving God as He may express Himself in our group conscience. Our leaders are but trusted servants; they do not govern.

3. The only requirement for A.A. membership is a desire to stop drinking.

4. Each group should be autonomous except in matters affecting other groups or A.A. as a whole.

5. Each group has but one primary purpose—to carry its message to the alcoholic who suffers.

6. An A.A. group ought never endorse, finance, or lend the A.A. name to any related facility or outside enterprise, lest problems of money, property, and prestige divert us from our primary purpose.

7. Every A.A. group ought to be fully self-supporting, declining outside contributions.

8. Alcoholics Anonymous should remain forever nonprofessional, but our service centers may employ special workers.

9. A.A., as such, ought never be organized; but we may create service boards or committees directly responsible to those they serve.

10. Alcoholics Anonymous has no opinion on outside issues; hence the A.A. name ought never be drawn into public controversy.

11. Our public relations policy is based on attraction rather than promotion; we need always to maintain personal anonymity at the level of press, radio, and films.

12. Anonymity is the spiritual foundation of our traditions, ever reminding us to place principles before personalities.[6]

Alcoholics Anonymous has had phenomenal success in its work with alcoholics. Many people formerly regarded as hopeless by doctors, psychiatrists, and loved ones have been restored to sobriety and a life of usefulness, dominated by a concern for other alcoholics.

Emerging Principles

An examination of these influential groups shows there were some common principles which seemed to relate to successful group life.

1. They were laymen's groups with professionals playing little if any part in the organization.

2. A spirit of concern for members of the group was a common characteristic.

3. The organization was loosely knit with a tendency ever present to consolidate and freeze into rigidity with a corresponding loss of effectiveness.

4. Each of these groups had high ethical standards. Both Methodism and the Oxford Group Movement were continually criticized because of their urgings toward Christian perfection. None of these groups advocated permissiveness or freedom from moral demands.

5. Openness through confession of one's own shortcomings to others was the focal point of the thinking of these groups.

6. Restitution or putting things right and trying to heal the hurt which had been caused is a constantly recurring note.

7. Each group laid a missionary responsibility upon the shoulders of its members to take the message to others.

None of these groups built an organization on carefully theorized psychological or sociological principles. Each arose spontaneously, as people with common needs and a concern for others were drawn together and devised principles which gave it an effectiveness out of all proportion to its size.

A socialization experience within these groups may be viewed from different perspectives and seen as presenting pitfalls or possibilities for the participants. The high ethical standards of the groups, with their insistence on confession of failure, easily marks them as arousers of guilt—a heinous offense in the eyes of a permissive psychology. But these very "provokers of guilt" have provided a modus operandi without peer in handling the troublesome effects of real or imagined wrongdoing. Their work provides a backdrop for considering the principles of integrity therapy.

5

CONFESSION: NEGATIVE AND POSITIVE

Psychotherapy and religion come closest to each other when they focus on confession. Like many of the helping techniques, confession was once the exclusive possession of religion, which either left it to be taken over by the new emerging and allegedly scientific profession of psychotherapy or surrounded it with a deadening ritual and legalism.

Many systems of psychotherapy recognize the characteristic human reaction of concealing the events of life which are painful to recall or those about which one doesn't wish his fellows to know. Jung gives an exposition of one of man's attempts to camouflage and disguise his past behavior.

As soon as man was capable of conceiving the idea of sin, he had recourse to psychic concealment—or, to put it in analytical language, repressions arose. Anything that is concealed is a secret. The maintenance of secrets acts like a psychic poison which alienates their possessor from the community. . . .

However beneficial a secret shared with several persons may be, a merely private secret has a destructive effect. It resembles a burden of guilt which cuts off the unfortunate possessor from communion with his fellow-beings. Yet if we are conscious of what we conceal, the harm done is decidedly less than if we do not know what we are repressing—or even that we have repressions at all. In the latter case we not merely keep a content consciously private, but we conceal it even from ourselves. It then splits off from consciousness as an independent complex, to lead a separate existence in the unconscious, where it can be neither corrected nor interfered with by the conscious mind. The complex is thus an autonomous portion of the psyche which, as experience has shown, develops a peculiar fantasy-life of its own.[1]

The dissembling, which has caused what Jung calls "psychic poison," has given psychology two of its most frequently used words to portray the finer points of concealment techniques. Both describe covering-up operations in personality functions. The main distinction between them is that one is conscious and the other an unconscious procedure.

Suppression refers to the deliberate mental activity by which the dirty linen basket of the mind is stuffed with the wrinkled and soiled rags of unworthy experience. The activity is consciously undertaken in much the same manner as the fussy housewife sorts the dirty laundry from the clean. This practice of evaluation against an ideal and conscious disposal is the distinctive suppression.

Repression, on the other hand, is an unconscious process. It bears a close resemblance to a socialite at a high-society function who, surprised by the unexpected presence of her maid who by some strange chance has also been invited, ignores the woman of lower social station, giving no indication of ever having previously met her. Freud spoke about the "Censor," a word having reference to Russian censorship which excluded all information except that specifically approved by the ruling powers. In similar manner, some experiences are consigned to the unconscious by an undercover operation carried on below the level of consciousness.

Once it is acknowledged that secrecy has caused many of the problems of life, the obvious antidote is self-revelation and openness. That towering pioneer in the study of psychology of religion, William James, noted this fact in his comments on the place of confession in religion.

Not nearly as widespread as sacrifice, it corresponds to a more inward and moral stage of sentiment. It is part of the general system of purgation and cleansing which one feels one's self in need of, in order to be in right relations to one's deity. For him who confesses, shams are over and realities have begun; he has exteriorized his rottenness. If he has not actually got rid of it, he at least no longer smears it over with a hypocritical show of virtue—he lives at least upon a basis of veracity.

The complete decay of the practice of confession in Anglo-Saxon communities is a little hard to account for. Reaction against popery is of course the historic explanation, for in popery confession went with penances and absolution, and other inadmissible practices. But on the side of the sinner himself it seems as if the need ought to have been too great to accept so summary a refusal of its satisfaction. One would think that in more men the shell of secrecy would have had to open, the pent-in abscess to burst and gain relief, even though the ear that heard the confession were unworthy. The Catholic Church, for obvious utilitarian reasons, has substituted auricular confession to one priest for the more radical act of public confession. We English-speaking Protestants, in the general self-reliance and unsociability of our nature, seem to find it enough if we take God alone into our confidence.[2]

With his usual perception James has gone to the heart of the problem. As religion developed historically, the emphasis moved from symbolic outward acts to inward responses: "Rend your hearts, not your garments"; "to obey is better than to sacrifice"; and "confession is one of the evidences of religion's inward nature." Rejection of a practice because of its use by the Roman Catholic Church is the poorest reason of all, and the action of enthusiastic reformers is sometimes described as "throwing out the baby with the bath water."

Even as the reformed church was turning its back on confession, there arose new secular forms ready to thoroughly "demythologize" the procedure and put it into an entirely new setting. The "scientific" new techniques of psychotherapy took the age-old practice and with appropriate accommodations placed it in their collection of therapeutic techniques. Jung openly acknowledged this when he said, "The first beginnings of all analytic treatment are to be found in its prototype, the confessional."

While working with Breuer, Freud had witnessed a strange incident in his teacher's therapy. A young woman being treated under hypnosis said, "Dr. Breuer, if you would only let me talk to you and tell you how my symptoms started, I think it would help."[3] Breuer agreed to let her talk. She expressed herself and felt relieved. They came to refer to this as the "talking cure." In the later development of his own technique, Freud devised his "free association," in which the patient reclined on a couch and expressed any thoughts that came into his mind in a type of freewheeling verbalizing and confession.

Free association continued to maintain the Catholic "one to one" relationship with the therapist, significantly seated at his "patient's" head and, like the confessor, out of sight. The analyst now became an authority figure of even greater power than the priest, as he searched the inner recesses of the patient's mind for the hidden repressions that caused his troubles. With an ex cathedra authority he pontificated the reason for it all and the patient was grateful to discover the "why" of his dilemma, even though he sometimes continued in his misery.

Probably the most powerful theory of all in recent days, and one which has exerted a wide and pervasive influence on the pastoral counseling movement, has been Carl Roger's client-centered therapy. In many ways this theory heralded a new day in counseling and was a healthy antidote to the tendency of ministers to charm glibly their counselees with verbiage. One of its chief virtues was that it taught the pastor the necessity and value of listening.

A critical examination of this theory may give the impression that it is the "talk cure," with the client sitting upright instead of

reclining, as in psychoanalysis. But there are some important distinctives, not the least of which is that there is no interpretation.
The skill of the client-centered counselor lies in his ability to
keep out of the way of free expression of speech and emotion.

Other movements also discovered the viability of openness.
Alcoholics Anonymous' fifth step is, "Admitted to God, to ourselves, and to another human being the exact nature of our
wrongs." The importance of this step is emphasized by the organization! "If we skip this vital step, we may not overcome
drinking. Time after time newcomers have tried to keep to themselves certain facts about their lives. Trying to avoid this hum-
bling experience, they have turned to easier methods. Almost
invariably they got drunk."[4] As one AA writer put it, "Confession . . . is medicine for the soul."

Writing about the means by which the various systems of
psychotherapy attain their therapeutic objective, Harper notes:

Another component frequently found in the psychotherapeutic
process is what is generally called *catharsis*. The release of
pent-up feelings, the revelation of emotional secrets, in the warm
and understanding presence of the therapist, are generally helpful
to the patient. . . . the verbal expression of these feelings sometimes helps to dispel them.[5]

The ingenuity of the therapist has been extended through the
bubbling out of free association, the encouragement of verbalizing in client-centered therapy, the hypnotic trance in which conscious control is reduced, or narcotherapy where chemicals are
called in to help the secret get out of its hiding place. All are
aimed at the same result of openness with the expression of emotion.

Although at first glance, the confessional aspect of integrity
therapy seems like more of the same—merely the reintroduction
of an ancient practice which in itself would be no mean feat—

there are three distinctive differences which make the experience unique.

In most other systems a primary aim of any type of confession is catharsis, abreaction, or ventilation, which allows the expression of emotion. Integrity therapy subjects may give expression to their emotions, an experience which is respected by the group. Any integrity therapist can recall tense moments in the group as sympathetic members have listened, hanging onto every word of a distraught individual pouring out his troubles. But this is not seen as a primary purpose, nor is it necessarily of any great value by itself.

A second difference is that integrity therapy insists that confession must lead to appropriate activity or behavior.

The third distinctive concerns the question, "To whom should I confess?" As may be seen in the accompanying chart, in most systems of religion and psychotherapy the recipient of the con-

GROUP	ACTIVITY	RECIPIENT
Protestants	Confession	God
Catholics	Confession	Priest
Psychotherapy	Catharsis	Therapist
Psychoanalysis	Abreaction	Analyst
Marriage Counseling	Ventilation	Counselor
New Testament Christians	Confessing Faults	Other Church Members
Integrity Therapy	Openness	"Significant Others"

fession is one particular person, priest, therapist, analyst, or counselor. Thoroughly trained and very conscious of his role, he will tell the "counselee" or "patient" to confide in no one but him. Thus he overlooks the time-honored therapeutic role of the group.

The subject has been putting on a false front to his fellows and now has the need to disclose himself to others. This is not an advocacy of indiscriminate confession but calls for confession either to those whom he has deceived or people who are representative of, or symbolize, them. A therapy group provides this background against which the exploration of self takes place.

Positive Confession

Confession may be thought of as positive or negative. Negative confession is the admission of failure and shortcoming while positive confession is action which follows from the experience. It is a type of nonverbal communication taking place through the new type of redemptive activity through which the counselee tells his story of a new attitude to life. Confession is not only made with the mouth, it is completed and complemented with appropriate activity.

Most techniques of psychotherapy have methods of handling guilt. One way is to reduce guilt by showing how unnecessary it is. Ellis uses such a technique in the following case, in which he is couseling a young man troubled by a past sexual relationship with his sister. The therapist commences by recounting an experience of his own and evokes the response.

COUNSELEE: "You really did? And didn't blame yourself for what you were doing?"

THERAPIST: "Not a bit, that I can remember. And still don't. For what's wrong with good, honest lust? Naturally, when you do what you did, that's taking it a bit too far. There are laws against it—not against lusting, but against actually doing something with a girl like your sister. And, like it or not, we have to obey such laws, in order to keep out of trouble. But if we make a mistake, as you have done, and not kept to the law, then it's just that—a mistake. But you're not necessarily a bastard for making it—just a wrongdoer who has made a mistake and who'd better see that he doesn't repeat it again. Blaming yourself, however, for making this mistake is not going to help you to stop making similar ones. In fact, if you keep on blaming yourself the way you're doing, and keep thinking that you're the kind of a louse who must keep making mistakes, then of course you'll keep on making them—because you think you must."[6]

From this perspective any acknowledgment of guilt is self-defeating and compounds the difficulty. Rather unfortunately this method seldom brings lasting relief. Like the unwanted cat which the householder abandoned in the country, only to be awakened the next night by a pathetic meowing at the door, past events have a strange immortality and cannot just be ignored.

Integrity therapy takes an altogether different stance. If confession is, as Reik maintains, "the acknowledgment of guilt," and guilt means "to pay," there is another step to be taken so that payment may be made. Observation of the strange behavior of some maladjusted people has led some psychotherapists to refer to "the need for punishment."

One recent writer has seen evidence of this need for punishment in people who are "accident prone." A study of automobile accidents has shown that 4 percent of the drivers were involved in 36 percent of the accidents. A similar situation has been demonstrated in industry. One company adopted a policy of transferring truck drivers who had the most accidents to other types of work. They then discovered that these same individuals had a high accident rate on their new jobs. Further investigation revealed they also had frequent accidents at home or on their way to work. Some investigators have concluded that the "accident prone" people may really be unconsciously inflicting injuries on themselves.

Telling the story of his stay in a mental hospital, Anton T. Boisen relates an unusual experience:

One of the things which excited me very much was the treatment given in the hydrotherapeutic baths. I looked upon it as a sort of punishment or persecution. I would go repeatedly to the door of the tub-room and ask to take the place of one of the men whom I regarded as among my friends. One day—I think it was October 27—when I went there with this request I was ordered to stop. When I did not immediately obey, three young attendants threw me down on the floor and began to beat me up, starting in the small of the back and working upwards. I was then carried back to bed. After staying there a little while, it came to me that I had done wrong in going back so easily, that I ought to have made them finish me up and that only thus could I release the spirit I thought imprisoned within myself. I went back then and was given a more severe beating. I can feel the effects of it now, even after five weeks. One of the older attendants told me later that I was given what was known as "the old bughouse knockout." As I was being carried back—for I was not able to walk—I had momentary consciousness of being once more myself. For a day or two I was not able to get up. Then on October 29, which happened to be my birthday, I seemed to wake up. On that day I was brought before the staff and my doctor remarked, as I was leaving, that I had done pretty well.[8]

In each of these examples the method of expiation is unhealthy and damaging to both the individual and his society. If there really is some "need for punishment," a system of psychotherapy must provide a viable scheme to enable the subject to get the matter under control in a creative rather than self-destructive manner.

Our modern perplexity is as old as the judicial processes themselves. The code of King Hammurabi decreed: "If a man has struck his father, his hand shall be cut off. If a man has caused the loss of a patrician's limb, he shall shatter his limb. If a man has made the tooth of a man who is his equal to fall out, one shall make his tooth fall out." This *talion principle* is found among many of the primitive peoples: the thief loses a hand, the adulterer may be castrated, the perjurer has his tongue removed. One authority quotes the instance of a man who killed another by falling on him from a tree. The penalty was for a relative of the deceased to climb a tree and fall upon the murderer and so enact justice.

The Old Testament has a similar theme, "Whoso sheddeth man's blood, by man shall his blood be shed." Or, "Thou shalt give life for life, eye for eye, tooth for tooth, hand for hand, foot for foot, burning for burning, wound for wound, stripe for stripe."[9] Later came the principle of restitution. In the case of stealing an ox, the restitution was to be fivefold; a sheep, fourfold; and in property damage, the simple equivalent was all that was necessary. Other instances were covered by the command:

When a man or a woman commits any of the sins that men commit by breaking faith with the Lord, and that person is guilty, he shall confess his sin which he has committed; and he shall make full restitution for his wrong, adding a fifth to it, and giving it to him to whom he did the wrong.[10]

John R. Scott points up the difference between the sin offering and the trespass offering, called in the Revised Standard Version the "guilt offering." This latter was a provision for special sins and these also had to be accompanied by restitution.

When one has sinned and become guilty, he shall restore what he took by robbery, or what he got by oppression, or the deposit which was committed to him, or the lost thing which he found, or anything about which he has sworn falsely; he shall restore it in full, and shall add a fifth to it, and give it to him to whom it belongs, on the day of his guilt offering.[11]

In acts of irresponsibility where other members of the human family have been hurt there was to be a process of "putting back."

Much of the discussion in evangelical circles has focused on whether God really requires penitential activity before the individual can be forgiven. It may be that we have spent the time thinking about God when we should have been concentrating on man. It is not so much the demands of God for his satisfaction but the nature of man which calls for activity.

There is a sense in which all sin is against God and only he can forgive the sins of men and women. But it is one thing for God to forgive and another for the sinner to *know* he is forgiven. So Emerson speaks of "realized forgiveness," which he says is "the freedom to be a new creature and a new creator."[12] It frequently requires some plan for "putting back" before we can experience "realized forgiveness."

One of the finest examples of restitution is found in the ministry of Jesus and the way he handled the case of Zacchaeus. Scott comments:

In the New Testament, Zacchaeus, the dishonest tax-collector of Jericho, stands out as one of the most striking examples of restitution. When Jesus brought salvation to his house, he was not content to add to the stolen money, which he resolved to return, the one-fifth that the law required. He promised the Lord that he would restore *fourfold* the money of which he had defrauded people. He said he would go further even than that. No doubt because there were many of his ill fated customers whom he could never trace and therefore never repay, he proposed an equivalent: "Behold, Lord, the half of my goods, I give to the poor." In this way he was willing "to make satisfaction unto all them that he had done injury and wrong unto." This man meant business in his dealings with God. He was beginning a new life through Jesus. He knew perfectly well that his lifelong dishonesty could never be forgiven if he continued to live on the proceeds.[13]

This is "realized forgiveness," and most people need to see visible evidence or participate in an act which gives them an inward sense that they really are made whole again.

6

THE PROBLEM OF THE SOCIOPATH

One of the most frequently raised questions about integrity therapy has to do with psychopaths or sociopaths, people whose value systems seem for all practical purposes to be nonexistent. Because integrity therapy has emphasized the conscience or value system, the natural inference is that an individual with either a low level of values, or a practically nonexistent value system will not be a suitable subject for this type of therapy.

Practitioners of integrity therapy have been ready to acknowledge the problem of the sociopath. As the word implies, the individual has a sick relationship with society. He uses society for his own purposes, living in the area of immediacy and gaining his greatest joys from manipulating others. The very nature of his attitudes makes it exceedingly difficult to generate anything like a genuine concern about his relationship with other people. Consequently, the use of an integrity therapy technique does not have a very hopeful prognosis.

This is not the dilemma of integrity therapy alone. Almost every system of psychotherapy finds itself challenged at this point. Few can speak with any great pride of the outcome of therapy with sociopaths. It is strange that some should have chosen these grounds to have criticized integrity therapy.

Even more surprising is the fact that although integrity therapy has been willing to acknowledge the difficulty of working with the sociopath, many of its principles of honesty, openness, accepting responsibility, acknowledging wrongdoing, being subject to group pressures, and learning to actively follow a new pattern of behavior may actually constitute the only way the sociopath can be turned into the pathway of meaningful living. The principles are the same, but the practice involves a far more intensive application in an environment that brings a constant unrelenting pressure to bear upon the deviant personality.

The discussion may be sharpened by reference to drug addiction as an illustration of sociopathy. Although at first blush, addiction may appear to be a highly individual experience, closer examination shows it to have awesome social implications. As Mensh says, "Unlike other types of personality disorders, the addictions illustrate a peculiar 'contagion' or 'infection' in that a special social problem exists which is not found in other disorders."[1]

The antisocial nature of addiction is manifested in two ways. An individual who is "hooked" is confronted with the stark reality of the high cost of maintaining his addiction. To get enough money for the daily cost of from $25.00 to $50.00, the addict has to snatch purses, shoplift, break into houses, steal autos, engage in prostitution. As stolen goods return only about a third of their value to the thief, it may be necessary for the thieving addict to steal from $75.00 to $150.00 worth of goods *per day*. It is small wonder the drug-addict has been referred to as a "one-man crime wave."

The second and even more serious antisocial aspect comes with the addict's realization that the only hope of making enough money to support his addiction is to become a "pusher"—selling "dope" to others. There is small possibility of a ready-made clientele, so it almost inevitably means introducing others to the practice. Addicts who follow this course of action initiate anywhere from six to ten other people to "shooting dope," multiplying by this many the number of "one-man crime waves." By its very nature, addiction spreads and multiplies, with the addict's using his fellows as convenient means of fulfilling his own selfish needs. If the term sickness is to be used, the addict's real sickness lies in his relationship with his society, sociopathy.

Many have attempted to grapple with this problem by using the latest advances in the fields of medicine, chemistry, and psychology. But this has frequently proved to be an expensive procedure. Some treatments cost as much as forty dollars a day, yet bring only scant success. A large proportion of the treated people lapse back into their former habits, bringing misery to themselves and relatives and placing a terrible burden on society. Many a sociologist or psychologist sadly shakes his head when questioned about the prognosis of the addict.

In contrast to the poor performance of many of the so-called *scientific techniques*, a fairly new venture has had a truly remarkable record. It is called Daytop Village, the word "Daytop" being the initials of Drug Addiction Treatment of Probationers. It starts off with a remarkable reversal of a hitherto basic idea of drug-addiction.

"The concept of the drug-addict as an ill person and therefore automatically entitled to the recognized prerogatives of the role of the ill in our society in terms of sympathetic understanding, special concern, leniency and forgiveness is vehemently fought as an ideology."[2] Addiction is seen not as an illness but the outcome of personal irresponsibility.

With this philosophy every activity of the enterprise is geared toward compelling the addict to become responsible. No effort is made to find the *cause* of his addiction. The addict is not permitted to blame his behavior on his parents, the school, the neighborhood, or society. Only one reason for addiction is seen—*stupidity*. Again and again the word "stupidity" is used to describe the behavior which leads the addict into his trouble.

The Daytop project is the outcome of a search by enlightened court probation officers for a technique which might be effective in the rehabilitation of drug addicts. Impressed by the efforts of Synonan, a self-help group in many ways like Alcoholics Anonymous, which has had considerable success with addicts, the venture was launched in Staten Island, New York. In the course of its short history there have been many ups and downs, but the outcome is probably more rewarding than other such efforts.

The Intake Procedure

Addicts are investigated by court officers and if considered candidates for the Daytop experience a recommendation is presented to the judge. It is understood that the court has no control over the operation and that the addict has indicated an interest in breaking with drugs and making a change in his life. It will be up to him to enter Daytop and to show his willingness to work on reformation.

Responsibility is the keynote of the total program. The addict is released, given directions to Daytop, and enough money for his ferry and bus fare. Arriving at his destination, he is left to sit in silence. He is ignored by former friends and acquaintances now living in Daytop. His introduction involves being interviewed by several conventionally dressed young men who appear to be everyday, run-of-the-mill social workers. The orthodox approach of sympathy and understanding is used. After a casual introduction they suddenly turn the direction of the interchange and start in on a "clean-up" operation. The confrontation is carried on in the language of the gutter. The usual rationalizations of the addict are relentlessly attacked and his defenses cut away from under him.

One observer describes a response of the interviewers.

"Hey, stop this garbage. Who do you think you're talking to!"

The two interviewers speak to each other: "Did you ever hear such s - - t in your life!"

"This dope fiend thinks he's inside another joint."

"He didn't get enough affection and love from his mudder and fodder, I bet."[3]

In the course of the discussion which follows, the interviewers make it perfectly clear that they themselves are reformed addicts. They have behaved in exactly the same way, so there is nothing to be gained by his usual techniques of trying to manipulate them.

The whole emphasis is on the irresponsibility of the addict who, no matter what his chronological age, has been living at the level of a three-year-old child. If he is to come into this program he must learn to grow up and accept responsibility.

"Did anybody force you to stick a dirty needle into your arm and inject yourself with milk sugar?" the addict is challenged.

"Was it your father or mother who insisted you shoot up?"

"Was it the tough cop on the beat?"

"Was it your girl friend or schoolteacher?"[4]

When the addict is willing to acknowledge his own responsibility and that his *stupidity* brought on his trouble, when he is anxious to undertake a radical program of reformation, he is ready to start learning to live a new type of life at Daytop Lodge.

Living in Daytop

All aspects of living are toward building up social and individual responsibility in the life of the newcomer. The addict's family must reject him and be cold toward him. If he returns home they are to refuse entrance. They are advised to say, "Go back to Daytop. Get lost. We have nothing to say to you." If he telephones or writes letters, all his efforts at setting up communication are to be ignored.

The addict is impressed with the fact that he needs Daytop. The statement is, "We don't need you, you need us." Once admitted, he is committed to a life of responsibility in a highly developed social situation, controlled by the other inmates. All former addicts themselves, they are skilled practitioners in the art of "conning" people.

I made my first contact with Daytop as a member of a team conducting an Integrity Therapy Institute. Two young men greeted me at the airport. They were handsome, clean-cut, and friendly. They informed me they would be my escorts to the "house." I tried to think of a way I could find out if they were addicts, but I might as well have saved my energy. All the men from the director and his two assistants down have been addicts. However, these men had been off drugs for a long period of time and now occupied positions of trust in the organization.

The main building of Daytop Village is a large multiroomed residence. It is old but spotlessly clean and neat. Bathrooms shine, with towels on parade in a display that would rejoice the heart of the most fastidious housewife.

Three fundamental laws dominate Daytop:
1. No drugs or alcohol of any type
2. No physical violence
3. No shirking of responsibility[5]
The new member is told many times that the group is antidrug, antialcoholic, and anticrime.

A new arrival is constantly reminded of his responsibility. It is repeatedly reiterated that he is like a three-year-old and might easily damage himself; therefore, he is not allowed off the grounds without a senior member of the group. Whenever he leaves or enters he must check with the entrance clerk. He is not allowed to speak to newcomers since he knows only infantile methods of behavior.

I have worked with addicts in another setting and noted the way they stick by the "code of the streets." In one group a member looked me in the eye, and then making a gesture toward the chaplain said, "It's us against you." Sitting through hours of

these discussions, I was frequently frustrated by the total un-
reality of the atmosphere. The group members were altogether
conscious that they must stick together against anyone who represented "authority." One discussion of values was easily settled
for a group member who responded, "My therapist says right
and wrong are of no importance."

The climate of Daytop is quite different. House members are
compelled to become honest and open. An observer comments:

The newcomer is forbidden to engage in the type of conversation that constitutes 90% of the verbal intercourse that takes
place in the usual institutional setting of drug addicts. He may not
express any sympathy for the code of the street, which calls
on a criminal to remain silent about the antisocial activities of his
peers. He is expected to apply an honor code that is stricter
in many respects than the one imposed at West Point. The law
of the street, which forbids squealing, may be appropriate for
dope-shooting addicts and criminals, but here at the lodge, we
are involved in saving lives. Any member who fails to assume
responsibility for straightening out a tottering brother is en-
dangering that man's salvation, as well as the fate of the enterprise. On this score, it is not sufficient for a resident to ab-
stain from violating any of the tenets of the organization. He
is expected to bring up at the thrice weekly encounter meetings a critique of a fellow member who may be careless about
such a triviality as washing his coffee cup in order to gain practice in informing the environment when a fellow resident is
thinking of leaving to return to the use of drugs. A man may
be censured for not calling an emergency fireplace meeting to
discuss the waywardness of a buddy who seems to be "in a bag,"
involved in morbid self-analysis instead of working for the
welfare of all.[6]

A crisis came through one man's giving another a pack of
cigarettes and then admonishing him, "Don't tell anyone I gave
them to you." At this moment a staff member entered the room
and heard the remark. In the encounter which followed, all

the implications of this couple's having a secret from the others were explored. As tough as this may seem to the outsider, it is an important part of the socializing process which has no place for "the code of the streets."

The Encounter

Three nights a week the whole population of Daytop musters for a ninety-minute session of encounter. This unique event, described as "the principal formal medium for effecting value and behavioral changes," commences with a gathering in the assembly room. The leader stands to read the names of the participants in each group and designates their meeting places. It is the prerogative of any member of the community to fill out a slip indicating his desire to be in a group with a certain other individual. There may have been some difficulty of relationship and he wants to tell this other person what is "on his chest." From these requests, lists of group members are prepared with constant triweekly changes so that no persons are in the same group for successive meetings.

I tried to look nonchalant and unconcerned as I sat in the dining room with my assigned group. A man led off with a blast of abuse at the Puerto Rican, his superior who had offended him by his attitude in a work relationship. To say that the statements of the offended one were candid would be a gross understatement. In a couple of minutes the protester was pouring out a torrent of abuse, shouting and using language that shocked and amazed my middle-class, seminary-sheltered value concepts. The Puerto Rican, somewhat more under control, responded with vehemence. After a period in which I had grave apprehension that there might be a fist fight, acid throwing, pistol shooting, or knifing at any moment, the interchange gradually became less offensive and the emotion subsided to be followed by a much more rational discussion. Like a forest fire apparently extinguished at one spot but blazing into flame in another, it was but a moment before others in the group were at one another's throats as the focus moved around and allowed prejudices, hostilities, and animosities to be vented.

A sponsor, observer, and participant describes the differences between encounter and normal group therapy:

How do these sessions materially differ from conventional group therapy? In the first place, there is no formal leader, but each group includes at least one member trained and experienced in this form of group interaction.

Second, the search for elusive primary causes for addiction, based on some alleged childhood trauma or deprivation, is hooted down as a waste of time and a maneuver on the part of the participant to avoid facing his problems.

Third, the resident's behavior, in specific terms, becomes the subject of discussion and criticism rather than events of decades ago.

Finally, every member is expected to react spontaneously on a visceral level, employing, if he feels the need for it, the crudest terminology and vehement verbal expression. The group concentrates on reaching a "gut level" with the intent of having participants react at a rock-bottom emotional level, rather than on the intellectual plane that is so frequently characteristic of conventional group therapy.[7]

Having been in a far more conventional group of drug addicts one week and in an encounter at Daytop Village the following week was like leaving a stylish, polite afternoon tea party for a street brawl.

The language of the *encounter* is made even more significant because of the contrast with everyday living at Daytop. In normal interchange this type of talk is absolutely forbidden. For the observer it is of interest to note the content of the gutter language. It accuses the offender of incest and sexual perversion and evaluates him by the criteria of "middle-class morality." The outcomes sought are in conformity with the same morality—"to accept the square values about the primary goodness of hard work, recent relations with one's fellows, concern about the welfare of his brothers."[8]

Along with the "gut level" encounters there are daily seminars in which there is frequently a somewhat academic or philosophical starting point. A quote from Ralph Waldo Emerson or a similar author may be written on the blackboard. The group is encouraged to respond extemporaneously.

Evaluation

At first I felt overwhelmed by the complexity of Daytop. My impression was that the master wizard of bureaucracy had been turned loose with a free hand and the intricacies of the resulting organization made a government department look like a Quaker meeting.

A cooler evaluation revealed that everybody had a place on the status ladder. The emphasis was on advance by merit, so that the person who "stayed clean" and worked hardest made his way up in the bureaucracy. Hard work is seen as the most virtuous of all human activities and, along with honesty and openness, brings new levels of status and position within the "house."

Every Saturday night is "open house" to which outsiders are invited. Thus the former addicts learn to develop their social skills. With progress there come wider freedoms which eventuate into a new integration into society.

What are the factors which make Daytop Lodge so successful in its work with addicts?

1. It has absolutely no place for the "sickness" explanation of addiction. No addict is allowed to blame bodily constitution or chemical factors for his trouble.

2. Every addict must accept responsibility for himself and is not allowed to use any of the deterministic arguments that his

environment, circumstances, friends, or any other factor caused his trouble.

3. In conformity with this pose of responsibility the addict voluntarily commits himself to the program with a thorough-going desire to do something about changing his life.

4. There are no impartial professionals active in the organization of Daytop Lodge. The board of directors has many professionals on it. Specialists from the social science disciplines are constantly observing and evaluating. However, the whole program is under the control of former addicts, from the director on down.

5. There are strong group pressures within the community with no "in" or "out" groups. Each person is compelled by his fellow addicts to go straight. He knows he will be reported if he fails to live by the rules of the house.

6. The whole procedure is both intensive and extensive. An inmate is under supervision twenty-four hours a day. It takes about eighteen months for the addict to build in his new set of values preparatory for a return to normal society.

It makes no sense to minimize the problem of the sociopath and the stubborn resistance he presents to any type of therapy. But there are some breakthroughs. Alcoholics Anonymous lead the way, followed by a whole group of self-help movements like the "Seven Steppers" with former convicts and Synanon with drug addicts. A self-help program like Daytop Village, with its rigid program of socialization underlining openness, acknowledgment of failure, accepting personal responsibility, and a heavy emphasis on action, indicates some possibilities.

Daytop and Integrity Therapy

How does Daytop Village compare or contrast with integrity therapy? First, a difference. The encounter sessions apparently function on the theory that expression of emotion by "getting it off his chest" will enable the maladjusted person to take a more realistic view of his situation. Integrity therapy, with its emphasis on behavior rather than emotions, questions whether vehement expression really leads to a more rational approach to problems.

While counseling with one professional man with a deeply imbedded resentment toward his wife, the therapist worked on this expressive, theoretical basis, encouraging him to vent his emotions—to work through his hostility. After a number of sessions there was no progress. In an evaluation session the counselee said: "Every time I talk about these matters I get more stirred up and annoyed. It seems as if the whole problem becomes more vivid every time I talk about it." And this is typical of a number of cases where the expression which should have reduced the emotion apparently intensified it.

It was notable at Daytop that people could not vent their hostilities except during the "encounter" sessions and to that extent had to learn to discipline emotional outbursts. Allied with this was the report that newer members were more vocal than the more experienced. The longer a man was at Daytop the more likely he would be on the "receiving end" of a confrontation. It could be the maturing process made for more emotional control.

A second distinction of the encounter from integrity therapy lay in the nature of the "confrontation." In the Daytop experience the aggrieved person pours out his charges, while the accused defends himself with the hope that agreement will finally be reached. Integrity therapy invites the participant to accuse himself, to tell of his own shortcomings and failures. One of the functions of the group is to insist that a participant not "confess for others." Some members of an integrity therapy group have their feelings hurt when they are checked with: "Never mind about others, we want to hear about you." This policy is one of the strengths of integrity therapy.

Apart from these areas it becomes obvious that the difference between integrity therapy and Daytop Village is of degree. In integrity therapy participants may be involved in a ninety-minute or two-hour period, once weekly, whereas in Daytop Village the process continues for twenty-four hours a day, seven days a week, with constant supervision, triweekly encounters, seminars, and probes—and carefully supervised reward systems of status advancement. As Dr. Bassin says, "It takes eighteen months to build a conscience in an addict."

In summary, it could be concluded from this and other evidence that the principles of integrity therapy could be as effectively used with the sociopath as they have been with so many other personality types. But this evaluation will be cautiously made in the knowledge that there must be a rigid and prolonged application which is generally not possible in the normal setting of integrity therapy groups.

7

THE INVITATION TO DIALOGUE

One of the perennial problems of psychotherapy is to motivate troubled people to seek help for their difficulties. There is a common insistence that until the prospective counselee is "ready" to take the initiative very little can be done to help him. When he finally makes a move, he may find the "expert" in his inner sanctum awaiting his client's approach, something like an attractive, highly educated, but aloof girl, willing to fraternize with the ardent suitor, if he will pay enough attention and bring the necessary presents. The client must seek counseling and continue to take the initiative with a counselor who frequently has a "take it or leave it" attitude.

In his "Characteristic Steps in the Therapeutic Process," Rogers heads the list with "The Individual Comes for Help."[1] He points out that this is a step of the first magnitude. It is generally acknowledged that there must be a certain amount of psychological distress before any help can be effective. But while this may be appropriate for a professional with his selected clientele, it puts the minister, or for that matter the interested lay person, at a disadvantage, for there are many needy people who experience great difficulty in making a move for help.

Integrity therapy provides one way out of the impasse for one of its principles is, "We became willing to *use* our new openness."[2] This is the beginning point. A person has an experience of openness and then proceeds to try to help someone else. Like the members of Alcoholics Anonymous who claim one cannot keep his experience unless he gives it away, the helper must become a missionary for the new cause. It is not just a movement of professionals but also of laymen, who have become involved in helping their fellows. Integrity therapy insists that its "graduates" take the initiative in reaching out to other needy individuals.

Let us imagine a situation wherein Jean Harris has noted that Lynda Smith, a member of her Junior Women's Club, has been absent for a number of meetings. Jean has more than a suspicion that all is not well with Lynda and so decides to call on her.

In answer to the summons of the doorbell Lynda appears with disheveled hair and wrinkled housecoat. After apologizing for her disorderly house, she invites Jean to come in.

Preliminaries done with, Lynda offers an explanation for her absences. She pours out a tale of woe—telling how bad she has been feeling and the ridiculous way her husband is behaving; then there are all the difficulties with the children. As she talks she becomes emotionally overwrought and breaks down and sobs.

When she has calmed down, Jean begins to speak: "It's all right, Lynda, I don't mind your crying. In fact I know that a good cry often helps a woman. You might be interested to know I had an experience like yours. I had terrible headaches, lost all interest in life, used to lie around all day. I was completely miserable. Like you, I felt everybody was treating me badly, but while meeting with a group of people I made an important discovery. I found out I was responsible for my own difficulties. I am not proud of this, but I was having an affair with another man and George knew nothing about it. I thought I could get away with it but at last realized something had to be done."

Jean pauses, then looks at Lynda. "You see, Lynda, I knew and my conscience knew. All my sickness was from a bad conscience which kept reminding me of what I had hidden. I finally told George, and after the initial shock he acknowledged his own failures, and in a very short time I was feeling so much better. Because this experience meant an awful lot to me I thought I should share it with you."

Lynda begins to ply Jean with questions about her illness and the medicine she took, and Jean responds, "That's really not important. All my ills were symptoms of my guilt. Is it possible that you have done something which is causing your difficulties and making life unbearable for you?"

The emphasis of integrity therapy is on acting out the role, setting the example for the subject. The therapist has had an experience himself and now he "opens his life" and recounts what happened to him. He takes a calculated risk, for the other person may not respond. But he takes the initiative which opens the way for an interchange between them.

The processes of communication in helping relationships have frequently gone in different directions. The pastor, in his preaching ministry, propagates ideas to his waiting, and hopefully, listening congregation. Aware of his prophetic ministry, many a pastor has almost come to think of his statements as the "last word." One minister, approached by a troubled church member, said: "Don't worry, I'm going to preach about that next Sunday. Just be sure to be in church." As long as the minister expressed his word there was little for his troubled parishioner to do except hide the treasured statement away in his life.

Partially in reaction to this impersonal and aloof attitude toward the counselee has come "client-centered therapy." The peculiar skill of the counselor lies in developing responses which encourage his counselee to verbalize his innermost anxieties. The counselee calls the shots and the therapist follows in the way the counselee leads. A change of direction has come; the counselee talks and the counselor listens.

Now comes a new process which provides opportunity for give and take. As Anderson says it, describing the integrity therapy attitude, "I have become concerned to enter into a dialogue rather than a monologue with a troubled person."[3] The relationship is a two-way affair.

A counselee may hesitatingly ask: "Have you ever had an experience like this?" The counselor can answer in several ways.

He might answer: "You are the counselee and what has happened to me doesn't really matter."

If his technique comes from a more sophisticated source he may say, with the correct inflection of his voice, "You want to know if I have ever been in a situation like yours?"

In either case the counselee finds his reach for help disdainfully rejected. He continues on in his loneliness and isolation.

Now we have a method which provides the setting for an interchange between counselor and counselee. It may become a practical demonstration of the highly theoretical "dialogue" so often discussed in theological circles. If dialogue is "that address and response between persons in which there is a flow of meaning between them in spite of all the obstacles that normally would block the relationship"[4] integrity therapy presents a setting for a dialogue at its best.

Most troubled people are out of communication with their fellows. Like a careless traveler in a totalitarian state, suddenly arrested, thrown into jail, and held incommunicado, the "emotionally upset" person sits in his "penitentiary" of loneliness, cut off from his fellows.

One very attractive matrón, once vibrantly alive, now withdrawn and anxious, said: "I just don't know what to say when I am in company. At first I stood or sat around, then I decided people wouldn't find any pleasure in my company and socializing was a waste of time for both them and me, so I just stay at home."

Her expression of resignation and inevitability showed her inner despair. The lovely home, handsome and blossoming children, devoted and successful husband, might, by an easy flight of the imagination, be seen as the guards of a corrective institution.

The counselor in integrity therapy comes as an ambassador from the home community to protest the condition of the isolated prisoner. He demands an interview, tries to raise the captive's spirits with news of fresh hope. Preeminently he carries tidings of members of the home community who care and await news of release. In contrast with friends who, though they wished to help, felt unable to reach their companion, the integrity therapist gently but firmly pushes in to relate to the distressed person.

There is an explanation for all this isolation. The therapist is ready to show that the present condition is a perfectly logical outcome of past behavior. But above everything else, the therapist brings the startling news that he was once in the same situation himself. Martin Buber refers to "experiencing the other side" as a factor in dialogue. The willingness of the integrity therapist to tell his own experience gives an indication of understanding at least something of what is happening.

If the therapist has never passed through an event similar to that of the counselee in his own life, should he fabricate a situation?

Unless he has lived a checkered career it is highly improbable that a therapist will have anything like the experiences of some of his counselees. Integrity therapy does not mean a pastor has to swap sordid stories with a troubled person. As Anderson says, "It does mean that we demonstrate through our own witness that self-disclosure and entering into dialogue and community, making restitution and righting wrongs, is the way out of trouble."[5] Everyone has had some experiences which, while not exactly the same as the counselee's, are certainly illustrations of his own personal irresponsibility and the ultimate aftermath of concealment.

The effectiveness of this "invitation to dialogue" can only be

gauged by the results when it is put into practice. One case
stands out stark and clear. An eighteen-year-old girl had been
in a highly specialized institution before coming to the present
hospital. Withdrawn and passive, careless about her appearance,
Hazel did not appear a very promising prospect. In the initial interview she showed a polite but restrained interest. But when
one of the interviewers told of his experiences in a hospital and
went on to relate an event of earlier days and its obvious relationship to his bout of depression, her interest grew. When
invited to share her experiences, she talked in generalities for a
while, then told a story about an earlier indiscretion of which she
was obviously ashamed.

Hazel went on to join the group and share her experiences with
its members. Gradually a change came over her. She began to
take more pride in her appearance, enter more meaningfully into
the discussions, and to make plans for life after leaving the
hospital.

The peculiar aspect of this case was that in her previous
experiences in talking with highly trained professional people,
Hazel had never uttered a word about her earlier misdemeanors.
In the presence of the professionals she was only willing to talk
about the superficial aspects of her life, but when another person made the gesture of opening his life, she produced the significant material.

A young man with a history of depression came to see a
counselor. He was very sophisticated in the ways of psychotherapy, having spent some five months in a private psychiatric
hospital, where at considerable cost he had had intensive treatment. At this initial interview he talked at length about his
symptoms, his parents, and other authority figures in his life.
Handsome and attractive, he warmed to his subject and became
more voluble as the session went on.

At a convenient moment the counselor explained the theory

of integrity therapy. He then talked about an experience of irresponsibility in his own life. The young man grew strangely silent, then finally responded by relating some unworthy experiences of his own. In a later discussion he said he had never told anybody about these events of his life. Why, then, had he told the counselor? His reply, "I talked with the psychiatrist and he said he was a man like me, but it was all so vaguely stated. You told me about that crummy thing in your life and I felt I could share my experiences with you."

It has become a practice in counseling circles to distinguish between the "presenting" problem and the "real" problem. The "presenting" problem is that which the counselee talks of in the first interview, and it is generally acknowledged that it may be a "smoke-screen" response. As the counselee gradually gains confidence in the counselor and feels he can be trusted, he goes on to produce the "real" problem. Until this moment comes, much of the time is wasted. Both Hazel and the young man were willing to come out from behind their respective screens when counselors were willing to become open.

Apart from everything else, integrity therapy speeds up the process of psychotherapy, reducing the time taken in building rapport. The counselor shows himself worthy of trust by making a gesture of openness toward the counselee. He says, in effect, "We are entering a dialogue and relationship of mutual trust. To show how I feel about this I am going to open my life to you. I invite you to respond." And human nature being what it is, the gesture of goodwill opens the way for what Howe calls the "miracle of dialogue" and frequently brings the response of openness and honesty and restitution, leading the way to health and adjustment.

Principles of Opening Dialogue
in Integrity Therapy

1. Integrity therapy realizes the importance of listening to a troubled person and letting him tell his story.

2. While there is value in a person under stress seeking help in integrity therapy, a way is provided for the therapist to take the initiative.

3. As early as possible in the interview the therapist looks for a response from the subject.

4. Only after his own gesture of trust does the therapist look for a response from the subject.

5. The developing counseling situation is not a one-way relationship of counselor to counselee, or counselee to counselor, but shared dialogue between the two.

8

CONFESSION: THE END OF MORAL EXILE

Our family has done a lot of traveling to different parts of the United States in an automobile, often involving many long and monotonous miles. To pass away the time, we frequently play games. One of the most popular of these is a game in which the player imagines he is some particular person, and the rest of the party ask him questions about himself as they try to discover his identity. The game is called "Who Am I?"

For many people, life is one continual game of "Who Am I?" In their anxiety to "save face" they have never admitted to anyone just who they are. A poet described such a person:

> Always a mask
> Held in the slim hand, whitely,
> Always she had a mask before her face—
> Smiling and sprightly,
> The mask.
>
> For years and years I wondered
> But dared not ask
>
> And then—
> I blundered,
> I looked behind,
> Behind the mask,
> To find
> Nothing—
> She had no face.

> She had become
> Merely a hand
> Holding a mask
> With grace.[1]

Real self-knowledge was not only the aim of the Greek philosopher who said, "Know thyself," but also of Christianity. Jesus repeatedly used the Greek word translated "hypocrite," which literally means an actor, to describe people who were counterfeits in their religious experience. Like the actor on the Greek stage—with his facial mask, padded shoulders, and high-heeled boots, projecting himself into his role, Jesus said some religionists were playing a part. They were emphasizing the outward ceremonial rather than the inward moral requirements of true religion.

Some fifteen times over Jesus charged his hearers with being hypocrites, covering up the true pattern and intent of their lives. At the heart of his accusations stood the warning, "Beware of the leaven of the Pharisees, which is hypocrisy. Nothing is covered up that will not be revealed, or hidden that will not be known. Whatever you have said in the dark shall be heard in the light, and what you have whispered in private rooms shall be proclaimed upon the housetops."[2] The authentic religious person could not live his life at the secretive level.

Jesus was in tune with the Jewish Scriptures in his emphasis. The Old Testament contains many warnings about the dangers of deception and concealment. A Hebrew word generally employed to describe the experience and translated "hide" or "cover" is used in other contexts; e.g., a veil covering the face, water covering the earth, and clouds covering the sun. Just as clouds across the sun change the appearance of the landscape, or the veil conceals plain features, or clothes give an appearance quite unrelated to the true person, people can be deceptive about how they really are. The Old Testament word of admonition is, "He that covereth his sins shall not prosper."[3]

It may be that this tendency to keep secrets has physiological implications that could in some way be associated with deterioration of physical health. This is the thesis advanced by Sydney Jourard in his book *The Transparent Self*.[4] He points out that women are generally much more open and willing to reveal themselves than are men. Men, on the other hand, are generally proud of their capacities to "not show their cards," to put on a front of self-sufficiency to the world. Jourard notes the earlier deaths of men and wonders aloud if this may not in some way be related to their difficulty in self-disclosure.

The very fact of secrecy may be of greater import than the enormity of the offense. A deeply depressed woman who came for counseling was initiated into a therapy group. She had strong religious convictions, but after initial hesitation began to tell the story of a life intermittently lived with scant regard for the ethical implications of her faith. It gradually came out that she had lived in the most deviant manner and been involved in sexual promiscuity, incest, abortion, and sundry other practices not approved by her religion, or for that matter by society as a whole. Then came a tense moment as she blocked and could not go on. She looked pathetically around, warning the group that the next disclosure was of an offense far more heinous than all the rest. She had visited a neighbor to drink coffee. Her friend sat and smoked and appeared completely relaxed. To the visitor it looked as if smoking must have helped to bring about her neighbor's comfortable attitude. The way prepared, she now made her disclosure. "I smoke." For her this was the most terrible of all her transgressions and the one she wanted to keep safely hidden.

The group included some sophisticated women over whose faces there spread a look of incredulity. But for the counselee this was the worst of all her transgressions. She hid in the closet while smoking and lived in constant fear lest her husband, sons, or pastor discovered her secret. To make this disclosure required the supreme effort.

Into the Arms of Humanity

Covering up, concealing, disguising, and dissembling have brought on distress, depression, and psychic disturbance. The way back is the pathway of openness, revelation and self-disclosure. Integrity therapy is concerned with the task of reestablishing social contact and building new relationships. Its methods are aimed at helping the client come to a right relationship with his fellows.

This therapy never remains a one-to-one experience. It may begin on this basis, although it sometimes starts out with two "therapists" talking to the prospective group member. As soon as the new member achieves a degree of openness, everything possible is done to broaden the base of relationship. Having had a long conversation, contrary to the specific time limit of much orthodox counseling, sometimes a therapist moves on to introduce the subject to another group member. Expanding socialization moves in ever-widening circles as the sponsor introduces the new member to the group. Here the initiate catches something of the group spirit as he listens to other participants tell their stories, their discoveries of weaknesses, and the ways in which they met their troubles.

When the client feels at ease, and the convenient moment comes, sometimes assisted by the sponsor, he may begin to tell his story to the assembled company and confess his shortcomings and failures. A commonly used motto of integrity therapy is, "A man is never stronger than when he is admitting weaknesses."

It has now become obvious that integrity therapy puts heavy emphasis on confession. In doing so it employs one of the oldest techniques of helping troubled people that is known to man.

Religion, in almost all its forms, in the period of its most vibrant expression, has stressed the importance of one of several types of confession.

The Old Testament incident of the sin of Achan is a fine illustration of the social effects of behavior. Achan's disobedience to the rules of the Israelites impeded the whole program of occupation of Canaan. Joshua's word to the transgressor was, "Tell me now what thou hast done; hide it not from me."[5] The incident became a parable of human experience. All the people were affected by his transgression and confession had to be made before them.

John the Baptist's ministry in the New Testament was marked by the people's coming, "confessing their sins."[6] Paul's preaching at Ephesus was characterized by unusual power, with the result that many people "came, confessing and divulging their practices . . . a number . . . who practiced magic . . . brought their books . . . and burned them."[7]

Among the early Christians the exhortation was, "Confess your faults one to another . . . that ye may be healed."[8]

The Catholic Church has put more emphasis upon confession than any other church group, but there has been a slow evolution of the whole concept. As is often the case with dynamic ideas, it has gradually changed, with the resultant loss of much of its effectiveness. Lindsay notes, "In the ancient church, lapses into serious sin involved separation from the Christian fellowship, and readmission to communion was only to be had by public confession made in the presence of the whole congregation."[9] Confession evolved into a sacrament of the church, functioning on a one-to-one basis. It was so mechanical that much of the value of the experience was lost.

Rather ironically, Protestant pastoral counselors have been not a little envious of the secrecy of the confessional, feeling people are more ready to tell the priest their story because of the certainty of confidence. It now seems that some aspects of this very secrecy, so much envied, may be the weak point of the Catholic procedure.

When Martin Luther raised his voice against the Roman Catholic Church, he did not reject confession. As Bainton says, "He looked upon confession as useful, providing it was not institutionalized."[10] In the later development of Protestantism there came a strong reaction against the Catholic confessional. Rejecting the role of any human intermediary and emphasizing the priesthood of all believers, confession was seen as being made to God alone.

A recent book, *Confess Your Sins*,[11] has a suggestion by the author, an Anglican minister, that there are three types of confession: secret confession to God, private confession to an individual against whom the particular sin has been committed, and public confession because of an act against the congregation or a group of people. To these, integrity therapy would offer a fourth—*therapeutic confession*. While the first three have their place, confession made to "significant others" and followed by appropriate activity is the distinctive of integrity therapy.

The Fine Art of Confession

The word "confession" has been used in many different ways, which vary all the way from Communist techniques of brainwashing, through police procedures of extracting self-incriminating evidence, to sacramental confession for the forgiveness of sins. Integrity therapy confronts us with an entirely different concept of confession and it may be, in part, because of these other connotations that there is confusion in many minds about the dangers and problems of confession. Some of the factors which call for consideration include the following, most of which are adapted from O. Hobart Mowrer's paper, "How to Talk About Your Troubles."

Confession is not complaining.—A common misapprehension is that confession consists in a recital of difficulties and problems in the present or past which are upsetting the life of the client. The talk might not really be much different from the type of back-fence conversation in which women indulge as they tell the story of the awful struggle they are having in the battle of life.

If integrity therapy is correct, the aim of a confessional experience is, in the words of Meyer, to "make sense of the nonsense." Spending long periods of time on the "nonsense" will accomplish little. The activity of confession aims at finding the "sense." What lies back of all this verbiage of complaint? Lurking in the shadows behind the all-too-obvious symptom lies the cause which needs to be discovered.

Complaining generally focuses on the emotions. The subject spends the time describing how he feels. An integrity therapist knows he cannot change the individual's feelings, so the question most frequently asked is not, "How do you feel?" but "How have you been behaving?" *Acting* rather than *feeling* is the focus of attention.

Much that passes for therapy is in reality a bath of self-pity. In not a few instances it might even be an emotional debauch. Some self-centered counselees pay their fee and feel they have the right to use the hour to wallow in misery, as they pour out interminable tales of suffering and distress. A magazine cartoon showed a woman reclining on the psychiatrist's couch and saying, "If only my husband would listen to me like you do." It undoubtedly would have been much cheaper and might have been about as effective.

Many a counselor has sat through long hours of counselee filibustering and vaguely hoped it was accomplishing something. Integrity therapy provides its practitioner with both a theory and a tool. The counselor says, "What you are saying is just a lot of complaining. Let us not waste time. Tell me about some of your irresponsibility."

In one group a woman began to pour out her troubles as she lamented all that life had done to her. She was somewhat shocked when members of the group insisted she stop her whining. She hesitated for a few moments, then resumed her recital of grievances. A perceptive member of the group commented, "Poor Muriel." From that time forward, whenever she started complaining, there would be a chorus of "Poor Muriel" from the other members of the group. The patient objected to this type of treatment and finally withdrew. My last memory was of her shuffling along in a luncheon line, clad in her unattractive hospital clothes, and pouring out a tale of woe in a fellow patient's ears. She had found listeners to her complaints but was just a hollow shell of her former self.

It is virtually impossible to change the circumstances of most people's lives, and even if it could be done it might not always be desirable. The subject needs to learn new ways of grappling with life, whatever may be the circumstances. Integrity therapy does not see any therapeutic value in complaining and, consequently, cannot accept it as valid confession.

Confession is not blaming other people for problems and difficulties.—An intelligent observer once noted, "It seems as if we are raising a generation of parent-hating children." Many of these attitudes are the harvest of years of sowing an idea of psychological determinism, telling people they are victims of others' misconduct. With this alleged "scientific" support it is possible, by the process of rationalization, to build up a very plausible argument blaming other people for failure.

Integrity therapy insists on personal responsibility. When husbands and wives seek counseling they generally arrive with a list of the shortcomings of their mate. After talking with a couple separately, the stories are sometimes so divergent that the counselor is left with a question in his mind as to whether he grossly misunderstood the first interviewee, or whether both his counselees are referring to the same relationship. Each from his or her own perspective has seen all the faults of the partner. Confidently pushing the blame on to the spouse, he sits back in confident anticipation that the counselor will join forces with him to make his partner over again.

In such cases, an integrity therapy counselor can say, "All right. It may be that your husband is inept and has failed to fulfil his obligations. Let us assume he has made 90 percent of the mistakes in this marriage and you have failed in 10 percent of the relationship responsibilities. Let us focus on your 10 percent. Where have you failed? Tell us about your mistakes."

As confidence grows in an integrity therapy group, the members zoom in on the blamer and statements are frequently made like, "Never mind about what others did to you. What did you do yourself?" Someone's reciting a tale of what all the other people did is halted with, "Forget about others. Tell us about yourself."

Much depends upon just how a confession is made. In even such an intimate matter as praying, it is possible for the petitioner to preach to his fellows while importuning the Almighty. A woman who thinks she is confessing may agree to tell her husband about an act of unfaithfulness, but even as she relates the incident she does it in such a way as to lash out at him. "If you had not been so inattentive this would never have happened." Her alleged confession is a technique for blaming him, thus is really not a confession at all.

Confession focuses on weaknesses rather than strengths.—An attorney noted for his success in selection of personnel described his interviewing technique. The vital question to the prospective employe is, "What would you say is your weakest point?" If the man were honest enough to acknowledge his shortcomings it was in his favor as a possible employee. To admit one's failures is probably the indication of a humility necessary for any real honesty and willingness to learn.

William James refers to confession as "exteriorizing our rottenness," and the failures and shortcomings of life are the appropriate subjects for discussion in confession. People in trouble do not generally need therapy because of the strengths of their personality but rather on account of their weaknesses. Outstanding capacities can seldom be improved, but weaknesses can and should be the focal points for consideration.

A successful hospital therapy group made every effort to pull aside the artificial front presented to the world and help its members face themselves as they really were. In this particular group they kept emphasizing that they were not concerned with the strong points of the patient's personality, that they could not waste time unearthing "hidden nobility."

It must be acknowledged that a mixed-up soul may take to bragging about his sorry behavior, and there is certainly a point at which this ceases to be confession and turns to boasting. If a member of a group recounts the stories of his failures with obvious relish and shows no emotion when reporting breaches of normal standards of decency, there is grave doubt as to the therapeutic value of the experience. In the peculiar sensitivity a group develops, he is likely to be halted with, "You're not confessing, you're bragging."

An integrity therapy group has also learned to quickly recognize participants whose apparent faults are virtues. Given an opportunity to talk about herself and tell what her weaknesses are, a woman will frequently say, "I suppose my main problem is that I am just too sweet and kind. I let them walk all over me. I should have stood up for myself and not allowed my whole family to use me. It would have been much better if I had been mean and ugly to them." The group hastens to point out that she is not necessarily reporting her shortcomings. They insist she go down a little deeper and examine her real failures. Many would give anything to acquire the virtue of long-suffering.

This attention to faults and failings is the strategy suggested by Mowrer, who believes in confession of past misdeeds and concealment of present and future "good works." One of his favorite expressions is "charity by stealth."

Because a man's natural inclination is to create a favorable image of himself to others, he has a tendency to boast about his strong points and hide his imperfections. If a confessional experience is to be of value, it must be exactly the reverse and focus on the subject's shortcomings and failures.

We do not confess for others.—Many people are willing to confess by telling another person's story. A counselee will sometimes look the therapist in the eye and say, "To be perfectly honest . . ." The only difficulty is that he is generally being honest *about someone else.* If confession is to be effective it must be about one's self and not others.

A man had been unfaithful in his marriage. Hospitalized after a car accident and feeling judgment had come upon him, he sent for his wife and told the whole story, explaining in great detail the temptations his female accomplice had put in his way. His former partner suddenly found herself facing unanswerable evidence in the confession of her former boyfriend as he carefully confessed for her, while, in part, admitting his own mistake. This is the poorest type of confession and really not worthy of the name.

Alcoholics Anonymous, with a wide experience in these areas, advises its member to take particular care in making confessions of infidelity. If the wife wants to know who the partner was the answer is, "We feel we ought to say to her that we have no right to involve another."[12] AA is saying, "We have no right to confess for others."

In a somewhat similar vein, theoretical discussions with students and other interested groups almost invariably reach the point where the question is raised about the dangers of confession. The questions generally center around the possibility of a story's being repeated outside the group, thus compounding the difficulty. Gossip is always a problem with people who build up themselves by cutting down others.

In integrity therapy there is the constant reminder that it is "integrity" and, therefore, all that takes place is kept in the strictest confidence. It is a calculated risk, but the risk decreases as the group members become increasingly open in their own lives. Consequently, most integrity groups have no observers, only participants. The risk of talking outside the group in no way compares with the risk of the secrecy within the individual and the problems that it brings. Moreover, the problem would never arise if the principle *we do not confess for others* were followed.

Confession is made to the "significant others."—The real crux of the matter is to know to whom to confess. It would be ridiculous to run around telling every person one meets about his transgressions. David Belgum has told the story of a young minister in trouble. In discussing to whom he should confess, Belgum asked, "If someone were trying to blackmail you about this, whom would they threaten to tell?" When the minister answered, the counselor told him these were the people to whom he should go and make his confession. Integrity therapy never advocates indiscriminate confession. It is only the "significant others" who are appropriate subjects for confession.

The "significant others" within a therapy group are bound together in a *covenant of confidentiality*. There is a specific understanding at the outset that no one will repeat anything said within the group. In some groups this may be repeated several times over during a meeting.

Group members become more important because they are learning to know each other as they really are. One observer of an Alcoholics Anonymous group in action says of the spirit of camaraderie, "No one feels self-conscious. There's no reason to. Almost from the beginning, a new member finds himself unfolding the details of his life with all the pathos, tragedy, and bitter humor that only alcoholics know. His listeners are sympathetic. Everything that ever happened to him happened to others. Every excuse he ever used has already been worn threadbare. Every lie he ever told has been told many times. And every hiding place he ever used for his whisky is already known. As he unburdens himself, the alcoholic begins to feel *good!* Confession, he discovers, is medicine for the soul."[13]

Confession is a willingness to come under the judgment of our fellows.—Some people are inhibited by the fear that if they become open and acknowledge their failures the person to whom they confess will not understand or will look down on them in contempt. A mental set like this comes from the expectations of the society in which we live. Part of the anticipation is for a person to be self-reliant and strong with no indication of weakness. Convinced with this idea, we often overlook the potency of a gesture of honesty in which weaknesses are acknowledged.

One of the common fears in the husband-wife relationship is that if the erring spouse confesses to misdemeanors he provides a club with which his partner can hit him over the head. For many years I subscribed to this idea. The statement generally was, "If there is not some reason why you should tell, keep it to yourself." I went through the embarrassing experience of watching a husband or wife deceive a spouse because I had encouraged them *not* to tell.

But in my counseling work one strange fact stands above all others. A wife in trouble would come for counseling and after recounting, often very convincingly, what her husband had done,

CONFESSION: THE END OF MORAL EXILE

the counselor would suggest the spouse might also come for counseling. Almost invariably the wife would look with horror and characteristically respond, "I wish he would, but he won't . . . I know he won't, it's a shame, but that's him."

As she sat in her misery I would say, "I know a technique by which you can be 90 percent sure that he will come."

The wife would look startled and respond, "I'm afraid it isn't possible."

I would then answer, "If you will go home to your husband and say, 'Things have not been going well with us lately, so today I went to see a marriage counselor. It becomes obvious that I am responsible for a lot of the trouble we are having. Talking with the counselor I am more than ever convinced that I need help. The counselor suggested you should come and help me!"

Whenever a woman was willing to follow this technique, it almost always succeeded. Her willingness to acknowledge her own shortcomings and open her life to her husband found him remarkably ready to respond.

When we open our lives to the judgment of others we are often amazed at their reactions. Within this matrix we discover ourselves and the strength of the interest of our fellows.

In *A Man Called Peter*, Catherine Marshall tells about a period in her life when the doctor informed her that she had contracted tuberculosis. During the illness she passed through a crisis of which she says, "Through many days I put down on paper all the things of which I was ashamed. Some of it I shared with my mother, some with Peter. To some people far away I wrote letters asking their forgiveness for things they had long since forgotten, or never known about. It took me days to muster the courage to mail these letters."[14] Catherine Marshall later had what she interpreted as a miraculous deliverance from her illness. Who knows what part her openness may have played in the process.

The age-old practice of confession is coming into its own again
and in the most unlikely situations. There are many applications
of a time-honored principle. As Jung says with a fine turn of
phrase, "In keeping the matter private . . . I still continue in my
state of isolation. It is only with the help of confession that I am
able to throw myself into the arms of humanity freed at last
from the burden of moral exile."[15]

Principles of Confession in Integrity Therapy

1. Because it is an easy but self-defeating tendency for people to
put on a front and not acknowledge who they are, it is necessary
for them to drop their pretenses, and this is best done by confession.
2. While confession may be initially made to just one person, it
moves out in ever-widening circles to increasing numbers of
people.
3. Confession is not made indiscriminately but to the "significant
others" in the troubled person's life.
4. Complaining or blaming others for shortcomings is not confession.
5. We have no right to confess other people's shortcomings but
need to concentrate on our own points of failure.
6. Boasting about our virtues is not confession, which should focus on our weakness rather than our strength.
7. Confession is an indication that we are willing to come under
the judgment of our fellows.

9

THE "SMALL WORLD" OF GROUP THERAPY

The literature of early historical periods is frequently rich in more easily understood symbolism, and none more so than the writings of the Hebrews. Of Cain, faced with the facts of his misbehavior, the book of Genesis records the accusing statement, "If thou dost not well, sin lieth at the door."[1] The Oriental image of a crouching animal waiting at the entrance of the place of refuge, ready to spring upon the hapless Cain if he dared venture forth, was a warning of the futility of his withdrawal from responsibility for his own actions. Cain's surly and evasive response to a later statement was, "Am I my brother's keeper?" Having murdered his brother, he shrugged his shoulders, adopting an attitude of indifference and irresponsibility toward his fellowman.

The attitude of secrecy toward one's own personal conduct in some unmistakable way also affects a man's relationship to society. Jourard states it:

In a poker game, no man discloses the content of his hand to the other players. Instead, he tries to dissemble and bluff. If he holds four aces, he tries to get the others to believe his hand is empty, until it is time for the showdown. If he holds nothing, he tries to seem as if he holds four aces in order to get something for nothing. In a society which pits man against man, as in a poker game, people do keep a poker face; they wear a mask and let no one know what they are up to. In a society where man is *for* man, then the psychological iron curtain is dropped.[2]

Jourard goes on to make the telling point that in the family where we would ordinarily expect the members to be open, forthright, and frank with one another, we often discover the most adept playacting and dissembling. An adolescent will frequently say, "If my parents had any idea of what I am doing they would die." Within this basic social grouping, where there should be the most mature understanding, there is frequently the least self-disclosure, leading to suspicion that makes many families only a pathetic parody of their idealized portrayal.

One of the paradoxes of human existence is the relationship between the shared group experience and the individual's responsibility. Paul expresses this contradiction when he says, "Bear ye one another's burdens, and so fulfil the law of Christ,"[3] and then proceeds to declare, "Every man shall bear his own burden."[4] This tension between individual responsiblity and the support of the group, provides the matrix within which an individual learns to keep the delicate balance of dependence and independence in facing the grim realities of life.

Integrity therapy takes a distinctive view of the communal aspects of human experience. Perry London has highlighted Mowrer's view of society:

From the vantage of its social implications, it is vital to recognize that Mowrer's concept of community is not an entirely consensual or cultural relativistic one. The commitment he demands as the price of mental health is not merely commitment to an existing group of men nor to an existing society; by implication, at least, it is commitment to an ideal group, to a potential society motivated towards its members by some hypothetical good, by an optimum, not just a norm. He labels this ideal the Judeo-Christian ethic.[5]

In a summary of Mowrer's use of terms, London says, "God is used to mean the idealized objective of society."[6] Mowrer's concept is the very antithesis of those who unthinkingly blame society for all the misfortunes which come upon man. He shows that society really has a constructive and creative role to play in helping the individual to reach his potential.

Whereas William James in his definition of religion said it was "the feelings, acts, and experiences of individual men in their solitude,"[7] Mowrer takes the opposite position and views religion from the perspective of the group. He says, "The main root of the latter term [religion] is the Latin word *ligone* from which our ligature and ligament come. Thus religion means, literally, a reconnection, a reunion, reconciliation, relationship—'the blest tie that binds.' "[8] Mowrer's plea is for a more adequate utilization of the power inherent in group life, and one of his favored sayings is, "We alone can do it, but we cannot do it alone."

But like Cain, there are many who not only feel they can "do it alone," but can also use their fellowman for their own selfish purposes. Of all the deviations from normality which confront the social scientist, none is so puzzling, frustrating, and resistant to therapy as the psychopath or "sociopathic personality." As indicated by the etymology of the term, the sociopath has sick relations with his fellows. Outwardly he may be a charmer, but his social graces are employed to exploit, rather than help, his fellowman. Personally unable to appreciate gradualness, living by impulse, seeing no reason to work for his living, and proud of his quick wits, he sidesteps all responsibility for his behavior and develops elaborate rationalizations by which to make others responsible for his own shortcomings. The normal processes of socialization have never "taken" with him and he fails to learn to respect the rights of others.

Although characteristically the sociopath does not learn new and socially acceptable behavior from experience, as Thorne[9] has shown, he quickly gains insight into relationships in social life and learns to manipulate others for his own purposes. In many ways he learns group dynamics all too well and gains a tool for exploiting the members of the group, as is shown by a psychiatrist's description of his sociopathic patient:

> After two sessions with the psychiatrist, Maurice gave up treatment altogether and took up gambling and white slavery instead. He was sent to a penitentiary for one year, during which time he married a girl he had impregnated. When he was released, he made no attempt to pick up his life with his bride but found new and different women, all of whom found him fascinating and filled with sex appeal. With his smooth attractive manner, he charmed both men and women. He became a salesman, for a while, and within the various contacts he made, men loaned him money and women gave him themselves. Then one day a man played his own game with him: he lied and cheated and took Maurice's money. Maurice said nothing to him, but one evening he calmly shot him in the back.
>
> Thus I met him, when he was thirty and appeared sixteen. Yet his eyes were those of an old man. His life had been one of waste and destruction, and now he had killed a man and was to pay for it with "not less than twenty years, nor more than his natural life."[10]

The tragedy is that this polished performer with highly developed social skills, like the espionage agent, apparently loyal and patriotic, but in reality working for the country's subversion and downfall, is operating against all the established "rules of the game" that give stability and moral strength to society.

A similar attitude toward society is implied in the word "delinquent," which literally means to be wanting in one's duty, to leave, to neglect. As Cloward and Ohlin see the main idea of difficulty in dealing with hard core delinquents, they state:

> The absence of guilt feelings and a stubborn resistance to correction have earned such offenders the label of "psychopathic personalities." Most attempts to reform them through clinical therapy have been unsuccessful, largely because it is necessary for the "patient" to have guilt feelings before customary treatment

leading to psychological reorganization can be brought into play.[11]

The guilt which comes from the consciousness of crossing society's boundaries provides the point of leverage for a program of rehabilitation. Absence of a sense of responsibility to society, which gives rise to a feeling of guilt, produces an individual who is the frustration and despair of therapists. The dilemma of society in handling these people is highlighted by Thorne: "The sociopath oscillates between prison and mental hospital, being considered too sick to punish and too well to hospitalize."[12]

Approximating the sociopath in stubborn resistance to therapy is the homosexual, whose puzzling perversion constantly bedevils society. A recent report tells of a new type of therapy.

A new patient willing to try treatment (even though he may be skeptical or actually contemptuous) is inducted into a group that meets once a week for about one and one-half hours. He may show up flaunting gay clothes, gay mannerisms and is almost certain to insist that he was born a homosexual and is happy to remain one.

The more experienced patients in the group immediately challenge both his ideas and his behavior. They tell him that none of them wants to be seen leaving the building with anyone dressed the way he is. They tell him that they, too, used to affect to the same mannered speech that he does, and they are glad they quit. Most important, it soon becomes clear from discussion of their own problems that they never have been truly happy as homosexuals, and know they cannot be. Their anxiety is infectious, and this anxiety becomes the basis of a desire to change. The newcomers soon adopt "straight" clothing. One of the earliest behavior changes that Dr. Hadden sees is a less mannered way of speaking. And gradually the group knocks down all the rationalizations that homosexual propagandists have devised to justify themselves.

At the same time, patients support each other with the reassurance of belonging to a sympathetic group. Says Dr. Hadden:

"Seldom have I seen stronger group spirit. After severe social rejection, the progress of any member in any area has a tonic effect on the whole group. And when a member begins to make progress toward a heterosexual adjustment, the group affords remarkable support."[13]

The power of the group is seen in the effectiveness of the socializing process in restricting the individual by building up and defining the limits of sexual activity, all the while supporting and strengthening him in his struggles.

As has already been noted, the ideas people have of right and wrong are "rooted in the social nature of man and the conditions of social survival and progress." Aware of the expectations of the social group, the individual develops criteria for passing judgment on his own conduct. When behavior does not meet group standards he will probably become progressively disorganized within.

A person in a state of inner disharmony resulting from poor relations with his society is seen by Boisen[14] as facing three alternatives:

1. He may appeal from his normally accepted group and primary loyalties to another group with lower standards. In a counseling session with a group of drug addicts, one of them began to speak about their loyalty to each other in a common front against authority. He declared, "If you could only get people in society as a whole to have as much loyalty to their society as we do to our group you'd have it made."

Gangs and groups of antisocial people are able to develop a strong sense of loyalty, as is seen in the "code of the streets" which calls for heavy penalties for finking or squealing. However, these loyalties are generally short-lived and temporary, with no capacity for any real self-perpetuation.

2. He can withdraw from society as a whole and fall into inner disorganization. Like an echo chamber, reflecting back the mes-

sage shouted into it, behavior, disorganized in the sense that it does not harmonize with the norms of an idealized society, is reflected in the inner disorganization of the individual's intra-psychic life. This condition is frequently referred to as psychosis or neurosis.

3. The troubled individual may learn to look with regret upon his deviant behavior and decide it must be changed. Integrity therapy aims to help the subject clarify these objectives and work on changing his pattern of life. Obviously this change is most easily accomplished through a group.

Group therapy has come to the fore in psychiatric hospitals, and like so many other significant discoveries it was introduced in the first instance because of the shortage of professional help. The most economical way of using the limited number of professionals was to place them in a relationship with a number of people at one time. In the outworkings of this economy move it was discovered in many instances to be more effective than prolonged individual relationships.

One psychotherapist describes what happens when a patient is admitted to a group of ten or twelve others:

> The patient learns two things the first day in the group. First, and most important, all administrative decisions will be made in the group with the exception of those things that require medical training to evaluate: drugs, physical complaints, etc. This means that all passes, privileges, jobs, trial visits, and discharges will be accomplished through and in the group. Second, the patient is taught that no group member is ever sick; instead, he is crazy. When the word "crazy" is questioned, it is pointed out that the patient does and has done many crazy things. The word "sick" is treated like a dirty word, and any group member who tries to use this concept is in for a rough time from the rest of the group. Finally, the patient is obliged to commit him or herself to complete honesty with the group, and no reservations to this commitment are acceptable. The patient is "dishonest" if he with-

holds important information from the group, either about himself or about other group members.

It is emphasized from the beginning that it is not believed that it is necessary to modify the patients' assets so that no group time will be spent in recognizing or in unearthing hidden nobility. Rather, it is suggested that any improvement in emotional tone will result from identification and improving of methods of behaving which are essentially evasive, irresponsible, and dishonest. Sooner or later the new group member reaches the conclusion that he or she is immoral by his or her own standards, and the group agrees. This makes it possible for the patient to come up with some concrete goals which involve the improvement of behavior in the desired direction whether or not the patient feels ready to do so. Usually some time is spent in getting rid of what we have learned to call the "I'm-too-good-for-this-world" syndrome. The group will never accept noble reasons for bad behavior, and the patient is forced to look at all the obligations and commitments which have been accepted and given and which have not been kept. . . .

Historical material is not sought for, although typically much is spontaneously offered and discussed. However, when the patient offers some reason out of the distant past for current feelings of guilt, the group denies the validity of such an explanation and insists upon examining current reasons for guilt which are assumed to be deserved. No group member can get the group to accept the idea that guilt is the result of an over-punitive super-ego.[15]

This is not just a group of people interacting with one another and wandering along any convenient pathway. They are following a course delineated by a carefully formulated theory. A number of functions are being fulfilled: (1) Responsibility is emphasized with the rejection of excuses like sickness. (2) There is an insistence on openness and honesty. (3) No time is spent with the patients' assets but rather helping them discover their own shortcomings in the light of their personal standards. (4) The classical case study technique of reaching back into the past for possible causes is rejected. (5) In this setting there is a complete rejection of any idea of an overpunitive conscience or superego. This leads in turn to a definite emphasis on personal responsibility.

To return to the Cain incident in the Old Testament, it is recorded that the punishment for indifference to his fellowman and murdering his brother brings the penalty of separation from his fellows—"A fugitive and a vagabond shalt thou be in the earth."[16] At the moment of this sentence the antisocial Cain becomes aware of the value of group relationships—"My punishment is greater than I can bear."[17]

The Advantages of Group Counseling

Is group counseling really superior to individual encounters? After spending many years in individual counseling, both as a counselor and supervisor of trainee counselors, I have become aware of a number of superiorities in working with groups.

1. The group provides a situation in many ways similar to the social milieu in which the problems developed: in the family, at work, at school, in relating to the sexes, or in the community. As Earl D. Marsh says it, "By the crowd they have been broken, by the crowd they shall be healed." It is possible to paraphrase this and say, "By the group they were broken, by the group they shall be healed."

2. Group counseling allows for better use of time. One counselor can serve six to nine persons in the same amount of time it would normally take to handle one. The counselor who spends six hours a week counseling six individuals can counsel twenty-four to thirty-six in the same amount of time. Similarly the length of counseling can be extended over a greater number of interviews without any further encroachment on the counselor's time and energy.

3. Troubled people are provided with an opportunity to learn

skills in helping other people. Group members learn to listen, accept, challenge, support, clarify, and comfort other members of the group, as well as assist them in planning what they should do. In the processes of helping others they are less likely to feel sorry for themselves.

4. People in the group who have lost faith in their fellowmen frequently learn attitudes of trustfulness and faith. There is a constant repetition of the "covenant of confidentiality" which binds the group. Many of them feel that life has been hard with them, but here is a group of people who really care and are concerned for them.

5. Group experiences break down the sense of isolation. Group members often say, "I felt that I was badly off until I came here, now I can see my problems are very small compared with others." On other occasions a group member will identify with the person who is discussing his problem and say, "You know, John, I have the same sort of difficulty as you, and as you have talked about it, I have come to see what I should do." By projecting themselves into the speaker's problem they are compelled to think through their own difficulty.

6. Sometimes they will learn to look at their problem from an entirely different perspective. One woman in a group who had been guilty of having a clandestine affair with a man behind her husband's back found herself forced into a conversation with a woman whose husband had been unfaithful to her. As they talked about the problem from these two entirely different perspectives, they both came to appreciate more clearly the difficulties which they faced and the part they had played in their respective troubles.

7. The group processes often "produce" people with unusual gifts of group leadership. Some untrained lay people become very capable group leaders.

8. It prevents the possibility of an emotional involvement

which will sometimes come when a counselor spends long hours with a counselee who can easily misinterpret the situation or take advantage of it.

Clients will often resist group counseling. It is apparently much more flattering to have the individual attention of a professional than it is to be thrown in with a group of similarly troubled lay people. Yet if they are sensibly introduced to the process they will soon learn its advantages. And the defenses against "anyone else's knowing" may be a significant part of the difficulty which they need to surmount.

After working with a man in a "one-to-one" relationship for a year the counselor introduced the client to a group. At the very first meeting the man talked freely and produced a lot of material he had never before disclosed, significantly adding at the conclusion of the session, "I never have told anybody this before." At a later gathering of the group he confided, "I need this group; as I sit and listen to the others talk I see myself in their experiences and come to know myself better." John Donne said it with no more sincerity but perhaps a little more aptly:

No man is an island, entire of itself; every man is a piece of the continent, a part of the main; if a clod be washed away by the sea, Europe is the less, as well as if a promontory were, as well as if a manor of thy friends or of thine own were; any man's death diminishes me, because I am involved in mankind; therefore, never send to know for whom the bell tolls; it tolls for thee.

How are we "involved in mankind"? Integrity therapy insists on the values of social relationships and never keeps counseling on a "one-to-one" basis very long, but as rapidly as possible introduces the subject to the group. This group is a microcosm, "a little world," which is representative of the larger outside world. Experiences in this "little world" prepare the subject for his larger responsibility in the world of everyday living.

Principles of Group Relationships

1. A man's attitude of secrecy about his conduct not only affects him personally but also beclouds his relationships with his fellows.

2. Individual responsibility and the shared experiences with others are in a constant tension which ideally is neither complete dependence nor independence.

3. Respect for an idealized society's rules is the basis of healthy living and the damaging result of indifference to society is seen in the sociopath and the delinquent.

4. The therapeutic group is a microcosm, "a little world" within which the deviant personality is both rebuked and supported along the pathway to maturity.

10

INTEGRITY MEANS ACTION

"Therapy is not a matter of doing something to the individual, or of inducing him to do something about himself," says Carl Rogers in a widely accepted statement. Like John the Baptist who appeared among his more orthodox and complacent brethren, clad in a camel's hair garment girded with a leather belt, so in these days a modern prophet has appeared in the mysterious land of psychotherapy practice. Clad in academic gown, he blasted passive and permissive techniques of therapy and called for a new day characterized by activity, energy, and enthusiasm.

The whole field of psychotherapy is rather vague, with its theoretical basis often ill-defined and speculative. No theory focuses on just the thinking, feeling, or willing aspects of personality, entirely disregarding the other two factors, but some have highlighted and paid more attention to one to the detriment of the others. The distinctive emphasis in one of these areas has sometimes patterned both theory and practice.

Man is ideally a rational animal and in his maladjustment he may become irrational, illogical, or confused. Consequently some theories of psychotherapy have had an emphasis on the intellectual processes. Albert Ellis' Rational Therapy is built on this basis. Ellis describes his own technique:

The technique of therapy employed with this patient is rational emotive psychotherapy. Rational Therapy or (RT) is based on the assumption that human beings normally become emotionally disturbed because they are born with biological predispositions which make it easy for them to think crookedly or irrationally; and because they biosocially acquire illogical and nonsensical thoughts, philosophies, or attitudes. Human emotion itself is conceived of as largely being a certain kind—a biased, prejudiced kind—of thought; and it is held that people can be taught to change their negative and disturbed feelings by changing the thoughts that almost invariably underlie these feelings.[1]

The underlying premise is that if the sufferer's distorted *thinking* can be straightened out, he can live as the rational creature he was meant to be.

Other therapies, and these are probably the most numerous and influential of them all, have concerned themselves with *feeling*. Propagators of these have sometimes been disenchanted with the intellectual approach, and consider man's emotional life the arena of conflict, in which he most frequently is vanquished by neurosis and psychosis.

Rogers describes one of the distinctives of his client-centered therapy:

This newer therapy places greater stress upon the emotional elements, the feeling aspects of the situation, than upon the intellectual aspects. It is finally making effective the longstanding knowledge that most maladjustments are not failures in *knowing*, but that knowledge is ineffective because it is blocked by the emotional satisfactions which the individual achieves through his present maladjustments. The boy who steals knows that it is wrong and inadvisable. The parent who nags and condemns and rejects knows that such behavior is unfortunate in other parents. The student who gets low grades in spite of good ability frequently fails because of the emotional satisfactions of one sort and another which that failure brings to him. This newer therapy endeavors to work as directly as possible in the realm of feeling and emotion rather than attempting to achieve emotional reorganization through an intellectual approach.[2]

The practitioner of these expressive therapies aims at facilitating the release of pent-up emotions by the process of catharsis, with the hopeful prognosis that when these expressions of hostility and resentment have been verbalized, the way will be opened for new constructive attitudes.

A counselor attending a small conference of educators was amazed at the outburst of a fellow conferee. He came to know the man as the conference progressed, and one day while alone together, the counselor suggested his newfound friend's statements in the meeting had been rather strong. The fiery-tempered one looked at him in amazement, "But I have always understood from you fellows that I must not bottle up my feelings and that I was following good practice by expressing my emotion." Many a counselor, pondering the outbursts of his counselees and noting their lack of progress, had had second thoughts about the adequacy of these "expressive therapies" in bringing about life-changing experiences.

While concepts are certainly grappled with, and strong emotion is often expressed, in the processes of integrity therapy the main emphasis is on the *volitional level of life,* causing it to sometimes be referred to as an action therapy. Noticing the emphasis on confession, the question is sometimes asked as to what is the difference between this therapy and the others which make use of confession. As we noted in chapter 5, there are some therapies which have a place for a form of confession, but here the similarity with integrity therapy ceases. The role of the group is one distinction, but the main difference is that in integrity therapy, confession is never just a catharsis experience primarily aimed at the expression of emotion. It is only one stage in an ongoing process which, if it does not lead to restitution and a plan of action, has stopped short of its therapeutic objective.

Mowrer is careful to make this point when, after discussing

the value of confession, he indicates, "There is no magic in admitting 'who we are' to one person unless we (1) progressively extend our openness to significant others in our lives, (2) take steps to *change* our behavior and rectify past injustices, and (3) become willing to use our new openness in a helping relationship with others."[3] Mowrer likes to paraphrase a statement by Stanley Jones, "It is easier to *act* yourself into a new way of feeling, than to feel yourself into a new way of acting." It was not just talk that brought on your problems and it is highly improbable we will talk ourselves out of them. Our difficulties are the direct outcome of irresponsible behavior and a whole new pattern of behavior has to be learned.

Victor Frankl, after his harrowing experiences in a concentration camp, reached a place where he realized life consisted in more than philosophical speculation. "We need to stop asking ourselves about the meaning of life, and instead to think of ourselves as those who are questioned by life—daily and hourly. Our answer must consist, not in talk and meditation but in *right action* and *right conduct*."[4] Seeing meaning in life, Frankl came to the awareness of what he calls "creative values." While in the Auschwitz concentration camp he set about replacing a lost manuscript on logotherapy. Although ill with typhus fever, he jotted down his notes and completed an outline for his writing. Activity, when there might have been resignation, helped to save the day.

Integrity therapy goes beyond the plain fact of activity to insist that the guilty person has broken the internalized rules and standards of society. Now in the commonly accepted legal parlance used of wrongdoing, he has an obligation to "repay his debt to society." He must do something, work at it, if he is to satisfy the demands of his conscience. Mowrer, with no faith in psychoanalysis or with the highly developed professionalism of psychotherapy, makes a tongue-in-cheek concession by saying that the sums of money paid by the client, probably came to constitute a penance in his mind, and payment for services may be the chief value of the experience.

Arthur Koestler, who wrote with such perception about the devious practices and forced confessions of communism, in his own personal life became a life-size illustration of the relationship of guilt and expiation. His biographer notes:

Koestler has been hagridden by a sense of guilt over which he has as much control as over a tumor. He belonged to a comfortable middle-class family which encountered hard times after the failure of his father's business in 1914. Thereafter he always suffered a pang of guilt when his parents bought him books or toys. As a development of this he developed a strong dislike of the obviously rich, not through envy but because they were able to buy things without a guilty conscience.[5]

Whether the biographer's interpretation of Koestler's guilt was correct is open to question. It could have come from any of a number of roots, with his underprivileged childhood as a convenient focal point for blame.

Later in his life, while participating in the Civil War in Spain, Koestler was sentenced to death and placed in prison to await the carrying out of the execution. Atkins notes a peculiar aspect of the prison experience: "Yet while in prison, in solitary confinement and under sentence of death, Koestler's guilt dropped from him like a worn-out cloak. There was indeed no longer any need for it. He was expiating his guilt to the hilt."[6]

Koestler, living under a sentence of death, should have been anxious and upset, but for once in his life he felt at ease and free from a sense of guilt. The experience he was passing through made sense. It was appropriate to his own personal sense of wrongdoing and gave him a satisfaction of expiation.

Similarly in psychotherapy a plan of action has been successfully used. A psychiatrist has reported on a technique for deal-ing with depressed patients known as "an antidepressant regime." The doctor commences by carefully explaining to the patient that there is nothing physically wrong with him, therefore his therapy is in many ways to be the opposite of the procedures for physical illness. Instead of instructing him to go to bed and take it easy, the plan of treatment calls for a program of intensive activity.

The patient is put on a compulsive rigid daily schedule. He is given as many nonrewarding activities as can be devised. He is to sleep less and not be permitted to take naps during the day. When he reports to the therapist, he learns he is not doing enough and must work harder. Explaining the reason for this demanding regime the therapist says, "What you are doing is giving him a way of expiating for his guilt in a constructive way."

Another therapeutic group in a mental hospital places obliga-tions on its members.

Upon entering the group, the patient is required to pay for treatment by taking on some work detail and can earn no privi-leges until work has become part of the daily schedule. Inas-much as the group members are the only permanent patients on the ward, they are given the responsibility for seeing that no work is done by the nursing staff that can be legally done by the patients. Thus they run the kitchen, the clothes room, all housekeeping details, as well as provide clerical help wherever it is then needed, and ground privileges are withheld if work is not satisfactory.[7]

In this manner the patient is given an opportunity to work off his guilt.

A woman came to join the therapy group. Her problem was her husband's alleged unfaithfulness. His partner worked in a nearby office, allowing them to rendezvous over coffee. When he

went off without his keys his wife chased after him to discover he was sitting in a car on the parking lot with his friend.
The aggrieved wife created a scene.

From this time on the wife lived in a veritable hell of jealousy.
She began deliberately displacing small items so that she would
have an excuse to run after him to work. On one occasion she
arrived before him. This led her to conclude he had been visit-
ing his friend on the way. The husband admitted a friendship
with the person in question. He not only vowed it was platonic
but undertook to terminate all relationships with the other
woman.

It was at this stage that the troubled wife joined an integrity
therapy group. Well dressed and nicely spoken, she found great
difficulty in telling her story, but through it all was one theme
—her husband was untrue to her. From the very beginning the
group bore down on the necessity of her facing her own shortcomings rather than his. At long last there came a story about
some deceptive activity in her past which she had kept hidden
from her husband. She verbalized the experience with difficulty,
but the group supported and encouraged her as she told the
story.

In accordance with the theory of integrity therapy it was
anticipated that she would get relief from her jealousy. She
was guilty because of her past deception and expected to be
punished by her husband's unfaithfulness. To our great dismay
she showed a slight improvement, then began to lapse back
into her former frame of mind.

For several weeks she missed the group, then made a dramatic
appearance with her usual careful coiffure disheveled. As the
group moved forward in discussion, she gave evidence of wanting to say something, and as soon as the opportunity presented
itself poured out a story of an experience a few weeks previously.

While driving down the street she had collided with another

car. In the awful, benumbed moments, she came to the conclusion that all her jealousy was completely unnecessary. She looked triumphantly around the group to announce she had her jealousy completely under control. The relationship with her husband was better than ever. Being a sincerely religious person, she thanked God that he had taken away her jealousy.

As leader of the group, I felt there was a simpler, human aspect of it all. In her experience she had faced herself with caution and difficulty. Gradually she had accepted responsibility for her jealousy. She then began to become more open about her own failures in life. One step yet remained. There was no *restitution* or expiation; hence, her difficulty. The terror of the car wreck brought her a sense of punishment and this supposed payment got her back on her feet again.

Mr. and Mrs. Goodhew, a handsome couple in their middle thirties, came for an interview. Obviously more aggressive than her husband, Mrs. Goodhew told this story. Her high school daughter was pregnant and would shortly give birth to a baby. The boy who had impregnated her was considered quite immature by the parents, and the daughter, now experiencing the same feeling, had broken up the relationship some months previously. The girl of rather slight build had carefully hidden her condition, but at last the secret was out.

Mrs. Goodhew was distraught with concern for her daughter. Terribly disappointed, she nevertheless took a calm view of the situation from the daughter's perspective. Realizing the daughter had no real attachment for the boy, the couple laid plans for the birth and adoption of the child. It entailed Mr. Goodhew's resigning his position and seeking a new one in a distant state. The lovely new home for which they had worked so long was to be sold at considerable loss so the whole family could move away to protect the daughter's good name.

Later the daughter came to talk with the counselor. She was

very much aware of all that her parents had done for her. But as the conference proceeded she said, "They are being too kind; they will not let me suffer for what I have done."

The reaction of the mother was in many ways kind, understanding, and Christian. But was it the best for the girl? It is interesting to note that she herself uttered a complaint that her parents would not let her suffer.

We were in a therapy group in which I was confronting a woman with the evidence of her foolish and self-defeating behavior. A little embarrassed by my insistence, a fellow group member tried to soften it by saying, "He is being very hard on you, isn't he?" Whereupon the woman replied, "I want him to be hard on me."

Right from the beginning of integrity therapy, there is an insistence on action. At one hospital a girl being interviewed as a prospect for group therapy began to display some interest and response. Her hair unkempt, she sat with her shoulders slumped forward. At the conclusion of his interview, the group leader made a few suggestions: Don't lie around all day like some of these institutionalized people. Straighten up your shoulders. Get your hair fixed. Her response to these suggestions soon became the indications of her progress.

Mowrer sees much to commend in the Roman Catholic practice of sacramental confession, and Catholics are generally drawn to Mowrer's ideas. Nevertheless, he has some criticism of sacramental confession which may be summed up. (1) He laments the "sealing of the confessional" which makes it a relationship between priest and penitent rather than the penitent and the group. (2) He sees that confession is sometimes little more than an empty prefunctory formality. (3) The penance assigned is not psychologically adequate. (4) Absolution and forgiveness are *psychologically* questionable procedures. The gist of our present consideration is found in the last two statements.

Lest Protestants feel too smug and self-satisfied and encouraged by this criticism of the Catholic brethren, Mowrer saves some of his most telling blows for Protestants and their doctrine of justification by faith. Mowrer (following Bonhoeffer) calls this "cheap grace." He insists that provision should be made for some form of restitution if people are to receive real benefit from the experience. The possibility of a more adequate interpretation of Protestant doctrine will be examined in chapter 12, but if penances assigned by Roman Catholic priests are not "psychologically adequate," just what is adequate? Like the Mikado in the Gilbert and Sullivan opera who says, "My object all sublime, I will achieve in time to make the punishment fit the crime," each individual must discover for himself just what is his own personal "penance" and undertake a commensurate program of restitution.

Some integrity therapy groups try to help the disturbed fellow member plan a course of activity in some way appropriate to his failure in life. Although apparently a modern technique, it has some overtones of an earlier practice described by Lindsay in connection with confessional procedures in the primitive church.

Certain *satisfactions*, such as the manumission of slaves, prolonged fasting, extensive almsgiving . . . were the open signs of heartfelt sorrow, and were regarded as at once well-pleasing to God and evidence to the Christian community that the penitent had true repentance, and might be received back into their midst. The confession was made to the whole congregation; the amount of *satisfaction* deemed necessary was estimated by the congregation, and readmission was also dependent on the will of the whole congregation.[8]

The decision of a modern integrity therapy group, being symbolic of the offended society and its demands on the erring member, thus seems to have a historical precedent.

Most counselors have had occasion to talk with an unfaithful husband or one who in some other way has failed. This man will finally bring himself to tell his story and to seek reconciliation with his wife. After the initial shock, she often is understanding and assures him it is all over and done with, and he is accepted. Yet the husband continues to have anxious feelings. In this and similar cases, we sometimes say, "His wife has forgiven him but he cannot forgive himself."

In evangelical churches which emphasize salvation through faith, a guilty person will make a profession of faith in Christ and be assured of forgiveness. But he does not *feel* forgiven. Again we say, "God has pardoned him but he cannot forgive himself." He needs to become involved in some activity which leads to "realized forgiveness."

Alcoholics Anonymous has two important steps in its program: list all persons harmed and become willing to make amends to them all; make direct amends to such people whenever possible, except when to do so would injure them and others. As one commentator on this step has said: "In some ways it is easier to straighten things out with God than with other people, but straightening things out with them is the clearest evidence of a new resolve."

The Goal of Integrity Therapy

Therapy is never an end in itself. As interesting as the process might be for counselor and counselee, it must move toward some type of conclusion. An outcome much to be dreaded is a counselee's not only failing to progress but actually becoming more dependent, limping through life as an emotional retardee and requiring the constant encouragement of the therapist.

The most desirable consequence of therapy is that the subject, having gained control over former unruly forces of life, happily announces he can manage alone and goes on his way.

As with other types of psychotherapy, there are short-term counselees in integrity therapy, although some groups insist on at least six weeks. This is seen as the minimum time needed for one to really grasp the principles and practice them in a meaningful way. Some counselees are regular for a few weeks, get their symptoms under control, and then drop out. These are not following the ideals of integrity therapy. Once symptom relief is obtained, they are content to retire from the venture and follow an easy pathway.

In its best sense, integrity therapy is not a temporary alleviation of upset but a long-term commitment. It is sometimes said that integrity therapy is the fastest and the slowest, the shortest and the longest of all types of therapy. Following the principles of openness, restitution, and activity frequently brings fairly quick relief from psychotic suffering. However, this is not the ideal. Even when symptoms have abated there may still be a long way to go. Patterns of reaction have been built into life for a long period of time. The counselee is constantly warned that it will take time to learn new ways of living.

Experience has shown that group members formerly in trouble but now functioning fairly well become very capable leaders. They can speak with great feeling as they say, "Sure, I know how you feel; I have been there myself." But it all goes much deeper than this. They not only help others but in the process they help themselves. Like the AA members who say you cannot keep your experience unless you give it away, there is an insistence that in helping others we grow stronger in our own convictions and function more adequately.

The price of meaningful living is commitment to the ideals of integrity therapy. It is never just a respite from symptoms but means entering on a new way of life. Commitment to the life of openness often entails a fundamental change of character structure.

11

THREE LEVELS OF INTEGRITY THERAPY

Theorizings about personality dynamics and systems of psychotherapy continue to proliferate. One of the constant complaints against so many of these therapies is that they do not work, and little is accomplished by the long hours spent and the large sums of money invested.

From the earliest days of its development, integrity therapy has insisted that practice must keep pace with theory. This chapter is an effort to portray the work of integrity therapy as it is carried on at three levels—in a mental hospital, in a counseling center on a seminary campus, and in a local church.

In a Mental Hospital

Galesburg, Illinois, has many historic associations. Here the famous Lincoln-Douglas debates took place, and some years later was born Carl Sandburg, the writer of his illustrous predecessor's most definitive biography. Surrounded by the ubiquitous Illinois cornfields, on the fringe of the city stands the State Experimental Hospital, where in a room of the psychology department a group is involved in a bold new experiment in integrity therapy under the general direction of O. Hobart Mowrer.

As an Eli Lilly Fellow in the fall of 1964, it was my privilege to take the weekly trip to Galesburg. They were long and exacting days, but exciting, instructive, and sometimes a little depressing. What follows is an attempt to describe group activities on a "typical" day. However, as Dr. Mowrer once remarked, "There are no two days the same."

The hospital group is a mixed multitude. Some members are discharged patients who continue to return week by week to help in the process. The commonly used term for them is "graduates," although they may also be called "therapists" by some leaders. They sit in on the planning and evaluating conferences in the late afternoons, and their opinions are welcomed. In fact, they may have as much influence as any of the technically trained leaders, and they form a vital part of the ongoing activity of the group.

Most of the people in the therapy group are hospital patients referred by a doctor or staff member. Qualifications for these include: under fifty years of age; not institutionalized; and, preferably, not paranoid or sociopathic.

A prospective patient for therapy is interviewed by two members of the group. Here the "graduates" play an important role. As they enter into a discussion with the new person, the patient is encouraged to talk about his difficulty. As rapport develops, the graduates relate their own experiences as patients, and how openness has helped them and ultimately brought relief, restoration, and clearly defined objectives in life.

If the patient shows an interest and makes a good response, he is introduced to the other group members and becomes a part of the group therapy process. The new arrival is advised to carefully observe the activities and that he will have a chance to make his contribution to the discussion at the appropriate time.

Minimum ground rules are laid down. One of these is the prohibition of smoking. Since the meeting place is fairly small and a lot of smoke makes it physically uncomfortable, it is necessary to have some limitations. But there is another reason. Smoking is often a palliative, and integrity therapy has no place for any means of salving the finer sensitivities. One of the leaders himself had an experience with the group which led him to abandon the habit.

When the group reaches a consensus about when people may or may not smoke, it is written on the board. Everyone is expected to abide by the decision. If there is transgression a correction could result. The thesis is that most of these people are here because they have acted irresponsibly and disobeyed life's rules of the game. This observance of restriction may be a beginning point in building respect for observing rules and acting responsibly.

A beginning feature of the sessions is the period of "hopes and fears." People in the group can please themselves as to whether or not they will participate, and there is no discussion after any statement. The leader speaks about his own "hopes and fears." When he concludes, the next person tells of his particular aspirations and apprehensions. If someone does not wish to participate he simply "passes," although this rarely happens.

Following "hopes and fears," the group moves into the more usual activities. Someone is anxious to speak, but the leader may call upon another.

Depressed Susan makes a pathetic figure as she sits with shoulders hunched, constantly sniffing and blowing her nose. She punctuates her tale of woe with sniffs and sobs and relates the way everybody is down on her. She is obviously making a play for sympathy. Some of the newer members show concern, but not the more experienced. They focus on her self-pity, and it is not long before they are using the phrase "Poor Susan." They tell her she must accept responsibility and not see herself as the innocent victim of the machinations of her family, neighbor, or someone else. At first Susan looks perplexed and not a little disappointed that she is being corrected by the group.

One of the graduates recalls that she had a similar experience and tells how the group helped her define the reason. She had been covering up or keeping something from the very people she imagined were persecuting her. She repeats her own story and then asks Susan if it is possible she has done something like this. Susan hedges and tries to turn the conversation into another channel. The group remains silent for a while. Susan appears bewildered and says she needs some new pills. She still cannot face herself for what she is.

A priest with a clerical collar and saintly face tells his story. He is careful to point out that being a priest does not mean he is sinless. He has previously spoken about other areas of his life but today his problem is procrastination. He has been invited to participate in an important writing venture, and has accepted. He brings a smile to the faces of his listeners as he describes the techniques he used to evade his responsibilities and his attempts to put the blame on others.

One of the group members asks what he is going to do about his problem. He tells of a plan whereby he and another procrastinator in the group have teamed up to check on each other.

Some of the "graduates" are very aggressive. To the newcomer, particularly one from a background of client-centered therapy, such activities make him uneasy. He feels that untrained people are forcing situations best dealt with in a more gentle manner.

Probably the most objectionable feature of integrity therapy is the unwillingness of group members to listen. They have a tendency to interrupt, to almost "cross-examine" a person. However, it is surprising to see how often their "hunches" are correct and how seldom it is that the subject is annoyed by the directness or the tenacity of the approach.

As the group develops, the members become involved in one another's lives. They generally operate on a first name basis and even get to know the families of fellow members. The spirit of community becomes strong. A graduate will tell the leader she has something to share with the group and will recount a situation in which she "goofed."

Group members will sometimes verbalize such statements as, "If only the group were meeting next week; I badly need to share my experience after Wednesday." Many relate how much the group has meant to them. One may say, "I don't know why I'm telling this, except that I want the group to really come down on me." Others are not only willing but actually happy to have come under "the judgment of their fellows."

The hospital group goes on through the day. It sometimes seems as if they are reluctant to be separated for long. After a two-and-a-half-hour session, lunch is taken at the commissary where, as likely as not, graduates, outpatients, and group leaders will gather to eat together around a common table. A leader may be involved in conversation with a group member who by word or gesture has given a "cry for help."

At 1:00 P.M. all is set for another three-hour session at which someone may claim, "It's my turn." Sometimes the group dissolves into tears and other times collapses into laughter. Differences of opinion may provide occasions for the expression of indignation but there is always a shared concern.

Time for adjournment comes—on some occasions all too soon, at others as if on leaden wings. The staff, psychologists, chaplains, leaders, and graduates gather for the evaluative session. Expressions and opinions are frank and open, but underlying it all is the sense of common purpose in this practical outworking of integrity therapy.

In a Seminary Counseling Center

Integrity therapy has a distinct advantage for use on a seminary campus because its theory coincides with many biblical teachings about the nature of man. It also operates under a number of disadvantages both theoretical and practical. The theoretical disadvantages arise from Protestant theology which is not sympathetic toward confession and penance, both of which smack of Roman Catholicism. At first glance they are sometimes seen as the negation of the doctrine of justification by faith. A practical problem is that theological students have an image of themselves and the ministry. This often precludes their admission of ever having made a mistake, for fear that it might "reflect on the ministry."

The Baptist Counseling Center, located on the campus of Southwestern Baptist Seminary, is listed in the telephone directory. Thus there is a constant stream of townspeople calling in to make appointments for help with their marital and personal problems. Until the time of the experiment with integrity therapy, all counseling was done on a personal "one-to-one" basis. Now the counselees are drafted into groups and a good portion of them stay for a significant period of time. There are dropouts, but not as many as during the "one-to-one" era.

Although we had dire warning in the early days that people just wouldn't go into groups, the steady trickle grew to be almost a flood. The groups first met on the afternoons and then moved to an evening schedule, which was generally more convenient. This opened the way for many men to attend. For a period of time we were faced with the unusual situation of having more men than women. The attendance leveled out with an average of about fifty-five people divided into six groups—three of men and three of women. One was for male students and the other female. The female student group also included off-campus teenagers. This gave the students a sense of mission, as they not only grappled with their own problems but also gained a sense of trying to help others.

The induction processes took place on Tuesday afternoons. In the initial interview the counselor followed the procedure suggested in chapter 7. Every encouragement was given to the new counselee to talk. Having heard him out, the interviewer tried to point up areas of irresponsibility by sharing a personal experience which had at least some parallel. Then followed a brief exposition of the principles of integrity therapy after which a response was sought.

If the counselee gave expression to a real interest, an invitation was issued to join a group. The counselee was asked to sign a contract, making a commitment to attend the gatherings for at least six weeks. To add to the impression, this was duly signed in the presence of a witness. A small booklet explaining the principles of integrity therapy was given to the counselee, who was urged to read it and return that evening for the first session.

The timetable for our activities gradually evolved. Following afternoon interviews, the director and trainee counselors, plus one or two selected "graduates" (people in therapy who were so improved that they helped with the groups), met for a supper seminar in a private room off the cafeteria. At this gathering one of the trainees presented a paper on some theoretical aspect of psychotherapy.

Discussion was not limited to integrity therapy. The theoretical bases of other systems of psychotherapy were examined and consideration given to points of similarity and contrast with integrity therapy.

At 7:00 P.M., the leaders adjourned to a classroom to assemble with the therapy group members. The first fifteen minutes of this gathering were given over to an exposition of the theory of integrity therapy. On occasions a group member who had shown unusual improvement told about his experience. As a general practice, subjects like psychological determinism, responsibility, openness, conscience, guilt, confession, restitution, and group interaction were the focal points of discussion.

The groups adjourned to their respective meeting places for

the remainder of the two-hour period. At the conclusion of the session the leaders gathered for an hour-long evaluation conference. These sessions generally found the leaders excited, occasionally a little depressed from a difficult encounter. One interesting aspect was comparing notes. The leader of a woman's group wanted to know what Len's husband had said and how he was grappling with the problems of their relationship. Hearing the other partner's reaction was always enlightening. This discussion often led to plans being made as to the way the partners should be handled in future group meetings.

Within the groups themselves we followed much the same pattern as in the hospital. It soon became obvious that we had heterogeneous groups. Several people had well-formed delusions; there were a number of very depressed individuals; and some, presently functioning well, with a long history of anxiety and depression. A good number had had electroshock therapy, and most of these used tranquilizers. It soon appeared that we had about as many deviations from "normality" as there had been in the hospital group.

As the news spread concerning the group there were many "cries for help." One couple made a weekly two-hundred-mile round trip. Others came from distant parts of the state to stay in the city so they could participate in the activities.

We had a constant problem of selecting subjects and there were generally more interested people than we could take. Periodically it was suggested to some people who were not participating that they didn't really need to come. One woman who did not enter the discussion but after the session remarked, "It was better than *Peyton Place*," was soon eliminated from the group. We kept emphasizing that there were no observers, only participants.

Wider experience indicated the value of having newcomers entering the group periodically. This not only filled the vacancies of natural attrition but also brought a new interest and a sense of an outgoing outreach.

The group was "leader-centered." The leaders had often interviewed the individual members and consequently had a ready rapport. We were conscious of the theoretical basis upon which we were operating and the whole flow and movement of discussion was kept along this direction. Yet there were many times when the leader was apparently unnecessary. On occasions of necessary absences other members took over and successfully ran the group.

Results were good, although we had no precise means of measuring improvement. There was a minimum requirement of six weeks' attendance but no maximum. As some gained relief from their symptoms, they moved out. It took longer with some than with others. In many of these it was a slow growth, with periodic setbacks, but we insisted they be honest and relate failures as well as victories. Some in the group have been with us from the beginning and provide fine guidance and stimulus for the newer members.

The counseling center had previously operated on an individual basis. A comparison of the group activities with previous operations led to several conclusions. (1) Many more people were helped. Some weeks as many as sixty participants were involved in the different groups, an impossible number for individual counseling. (2) We did not need as large a professional staff. (3) It was not nearly as time-consuming. (4) Some members of the group rapidly developed considerable skill in acting as catalysts within the group. Even though they did not always have their own problems completely under control, they exercised a powerful influence on other participants. (5) There was generally rapt attention to all the proceedings as members projected themselves into the contributor's situation.

Altogether the group technique was infinitely superior to the previous "one-to-one" activity. The center now carries on the main thrust of its work on a group basis.

A Church Group

It has been my hope that integrity therapy would spread to local churches. Whenever a pastor comes to, or calls, the counseling center to make an appointment for one of his flock, he is invited to accompany his parishioner to see the practical out-workings of integrity therapy. The hopeful outcome of this procedure would be the minister's return to his church, to form a small group built around himself and his parishioner, and then reach out a helping hand to other needy people within this particular church fellowship.

The church group within which I worked started with a distinct disadvantage. While speaking at a conference I was asked about integrity therapy, and in a moment of enthusiasm agreed to commence a group if as many as eight participants could be found. There was a ready response and the group launched itself on the sea of self-understanding without a really adequate preparation.

One obvious problem in a group associated with a small church is that the participants know each other so well. In this situation there was a reticence to speak and a concern about the response of the other group members. It was a mixed gathering with women in the majority. One husband and wife came together and at times a healthy dialogue developed between them. There was a certain uneasiness on the part of some of the women. The pastor commented that very few of them really seemed to "open up." Only on a few occasions did they achieve anything like the openness of the counseling center group.

An early experience seemed to confirm the fears of apprehensive participants. A personable man who had been drinking secretly told of his difficulties and was apparently helped by the experience of sharing his problem. The following Sunday he turned up at a church meeting intoxicated and proceeded to talk very freely. There were uneasy moments among the members of the therapy group as they waited in horror for him to repeat what had been said in the meeting. The happy sequel was that he faced his problem and went to Alcoholics Anonymous and thus started on a new pathway to controlling his drinking. It certainly seemed as if his initial experiences in integrity therapy paved the way for entry into AA.

Problems of gossip were raised by the inebriated participant. These possibilities are generally not nearly as real as some people anticipate but elementary precautions should be taken. Right from the beginning the idea of integrity needs underlining to indicate that a person trying to be honest, open, and committed to the group should never repeat anything verbalized in the sessions. It should be constantly emphasized that we do not confess for someone else. An individual tells his *own* story. Any indication of gossip must be faced and corrected immediately.

The group was launched amid the nervous chatter of people talking rapidly to cover up their apprehensions. After an introduction by the pastor I handed out copies of the booklet *Integrity Therapy*. With this in hand, I led a discussion of the principles upon which we would build our relationship. There were a few questions. The pastor tried to make up for his parishioners' reticence. I then told the group about an experience in my life as I tried to "model" the role I wanted them to play.

The response came slowly and hesitantly. It took several weeks for the barriers to be gradually lowered and the group to function with some degree of openness and freedom.

The minister had a deep love of people and was anxious to discover more effective ways to extend his helping ministry. Open and frank, he soon became competent as a leader. In personal evaluative discussions, he revealed that in trying to set an example before the group, he had opened his own life and told about incidents concealed for years. The telling of these things before his own church people had helped him.

One evening the minister confessed to a mistake he had made the previous Sunday. It was encouraging to see the reaction of church members who had heard of the event and now sympathetically responded to his acknowledgment of failure. The pastor felt he had grown emotionally through his own experience with the group. He stated his own benefit would have been enough justification for the time spent in the experiment. However, he was careful to indicate that there had been progress in the members of the group which continued to function for some time.

A church setting provides a natural opportunity for stressing a religious interpretation of integrity therapy. Reference to chapter 12 will indicate the biblical basis of principles used in the process. Many biblical illustrations could be used to show the outworking of integrity therapy. A church organization, called a Bible Mental Health Group, could meet on a Sunday evening, either before or after church, or on any other convenient occasion, fitting readily into the educational framework of church life.

As in other settings, if integrity therapy is to function adequately in a church there must be preparation. A minimum requirement would be at least one preliminary interview, with the pastor entering into dialogue with his troubled parishioner, inviting a response, expounding the fundamental principles, and so preparing the way for induction into the group.

Conclusion

After working integrity therapy at the three levels—mental hospital, seminary counseling center, and in a local church—some ideas begin to jell.

It is obvious that human influences and reactions are much the same in whatever setting they take place. The group in the counseling center had members just as "abnormal" as many in the mental hospital. I could not help but feel that if they had lived in close proximity to a hospital or had "knowledgeable" professional friends, they might have just as legitimately been "committed" with all the possibilities of settling into institutional life.

The large number in the seminary group who had electro-shock therapy and were now in about the same condition as before the experience, raised questions. Moreover, the large group of people taking the tranquilizers and compulsively continuing because of fear that if they stopped "something might happen," seriously raised the question of the validity of treating symptoms.

The supportive power of the group was of tremendous importance in each setting. It raises the obvious question as to why the modern church, committed to the use of small groups for administration and educational purposes, has not more enthusiastically seized hold of this technique for helping troubled people.

After so many hours of futility and frustration in nebulous and uncertain counseling activities and rationalizations about the failure to get anywhere, now comes a method that is simple, easy to use, and very productive.

There are no shortcuts in integrity therapy. The basic principles are clear. If these principles are followed through with the precautions indicated earlier, integrity therapy should be just as effective, no matter what the setting. We have the abiding conviction that it works—really works!

12

INTEGRITY THERAPY AND THE CHURCH

Many a thoughtful minister must have pondered the problems of his role in a modern society. Once, at least one of if not *the* best educated man in the town, he had his fingers in many pies. Gradually there arose new helping professions. First came the schoolteacher to take over his educational work; then came the social worker, specialized in meeting the problems of delinquency, drunkenness, and divorce; and then the psychologist and psychiatrist, who were looked to as the specialists in helping emotionally troubled people.

The puzzled minister, concerned about his relationships with the folk of his church and community, has the feeling that specialists with "scientific" training have taken all the functions which were formerly his special province.

In an effort to meet this challenge, new techniques of training ministers have been developed. It has been estimated that some twenty-five hundred ministers have had periods of clinical training within the walls of general and mental hospitals in the main, and spreading to other institutions of more recent days. The results of this training have not always been encouraging, for rather than defining the minister's distinctive role it has tended to make him a little ashamed of his old-fashioned profession.

While attending a conference of pastoral counselors the discussion centered around the work of an ordained minister participating in a chaplaincy training program. Before us was a verbatum report of the minister's conference with a woman patient in a general hospital. As the word-by-word account of the encounter was read, it soon became obvious that the woman, conscious she was talking to a minister, tried to raise issues about her religious faith. The minister showed the fruit of his training by adroitly sidestepping all religious conversation. He had the hallmarks of an amateur secular psychiatrist, with his distinctive religious experience and training playing little part in the helping process.

The man who might fairly be called the "Father of Clinical Pastoral Education" is Anton T. Boisen. In his biography he tells of his personal misgivings concerning the movement which he pioneered.

This meant that there was a tendency to accept Freudian doctrine on authority without scrutinizing it closely, and a failure to ask the questions which are of first importance to the student of religion. What is more, there was no attempt to develop methods of cooperative inquiry which would stand up under criticism nor to build up a body of tested and organized experience. The movement as a whole was not being undergirded by the program of inquiry which seemed to me so important.

I was especially troubled by a tendency to accept the easy solutions to some of the perennial problems of sin and salvation. Take, for example, a patient who is torn with conflict between the demands of conscience and his erotic desires and impulses. The solution offered by some of our chaplain-supervisors was that of getting rid of the conflict by lowering the conscience threshold. There were even those who accepted the later teachings of Wilhelm Reich, advocating a freedom quite at variance with the basic insights of the Hebrew-Christian religion.[1]

It seems as if these fears had a pretty sound basis, as may be observed in many of the pronouncements in experiences on clinical pastoral education.

Integrity therapy invites the minister to function in the role which should be his most important as far as men are concerned. Anderson states it: "The minister . . . is . . . recalled to an ancient role of being an 'expert' in morals, the resolution of guilt, and the reconciliation of estranged persons to the community and to God."[2]

After discussion of the basic ideas of integrity therapy, a thoughtful minister said: "Tonight a psychologist has reminded me that men and women are sinners, and that guilt is a grave reality with which they struggle. I was becoming a bit ashamed of this basic Christian idea and saying little about it." Integrity therapy insists that moral values are of primary importance.

The church is being recalled to its task as the conscience of society. A "clinically trained" minister who was trying to run his church on a psychological basis complained that a psychiatrist in his city "saw the church as a gigantic superego." The minister boldly asserted that the church has no right to make anybody feel guilty.

A secular psychologist, asked what the churches were doing about the recent upsurge of pornographic literature, complaining that he had not heard a single sermon on the subject. While he might have attended the wrong church, there can be no doubt that ministers are increasingly cautious about speaking out on moral issues. Integrity therapy reminds the church of its responsibility for moral standards and making obvious to a confused society what is right and wrong.

Integrity therapy also recalls us to the doctrine of the priesthood of all believers. Professionalism has sometimes blocked the way of people seeking help. The new and rising "self-help" movements are functioning with lay personnel, and Alcoholics Anonymous has displayed therapeutic vitality known to few institutions. In a democracy with a belief in the common man there are infinite possibilities of involving numbers of sensitive and concerned people in helping their fellows. The simple procedures and group activities are within the grasp of most ordinary people. A wide-awake church can enlist its membership in the ongoing enterprise.

In one training program for pastoral counselors several of the trainees were dropped from the group because of moral indiscretions. At a rather grim and soul-searching conference, one of the counselors remarked, "There seems to be an occupational hazard in this type of work."

Headlines in newspapers a few years ago told of a minister's admitting to an improper relationship. He had gone to bed with a woman, and while there the woman's husband, along with an accomplice, had jumped out of a closet and taken pictures of the situation, then proceeded to blackmail the minister. Further statements revealed that the woman, a former prostitute, had gone to the minister for help and had been in counseling for a year. It was interesting to see who had influenced whom, and to hear the woman's strange comment. When charged with blackmail she responded, "I love him."

The one-to-one relationship can easily create another "secret" which will further complicate life for both counselor and counselee. Integrity therapy stops this situation before it begins and provides a setting devoid of these pitfalls.

Mowrer describes the situation: "I believe there is rarely any need for a therapist and patient to have more than two or three private interviews, which should then lead into more intimate conversation with an expanding circle of other "growing persons" and relatively rapid introduction into a therapeutic community which will encourage and support the individual while he or she restructures and improves the quality of his relationship with 'significant others' and society in general."[3]

How does integrity therapy measure up to the standard of biblical revelation? Perry London comments on Mowrer's formulations: "Deliberately and lucidly, he employs conventional

theological language to describe (thoroughy secular concepts) and
thus endeared to the clergy, he proceeds to assault choice parts

EXPERIENCE	SCRIPTURE STATEMENT	REFERENCE
Human failure	There is no difference: For all have sinned, and come short of the glory of God.	Romans 3:22-23
Responsibility	So then every one of us shall give account of himself to God.	Romans 14:12
Conscience	The Gentiles, which have not the law . . . are a law unto themselves: Which shew the work of the law written on their hearts, their conscience also bearing witness.	Romans 2:14-15
Concealment	When I kept silence, my bones waxed old through my roaring all the day long.	Psalm 32:3
Parading virtue	And why beholdest thou the mote that is in thy brother's eye, but considerest not the beam that is in thine own eye? Or how wilt thou say to thy brother, Let me pull out the mote out of thine eye; and, behold, a beam is in thine own eye? Thou hypocrite, first cast out the beam out of thine own eye; and then shalt thou see clearly to cast out the mote out of thy brother's eye.	Matthew 7:3-5
Confession	He that covereth his sins shall not prosper: but whoso confesseth and forsaketh them shall have mercy.	Proverbs 28:13
Relationships	If thou bring thy gift to the altar, and there rememberest that thy brother hath ought against thee; leave there thy gift before the altar, and go thy way; first be reconciled to thy brother, and then come and offer thy gift.	Matthew 5:23-24

EXPERIENCE	SCRIPTURE STATEMENT	REFERENCE
Sharing	Confess your faults one to another.	James 5:16
Activity of faith	Your work of faith.	1 Thess. 1:3
	Fight the good fight of faith.	1 Timothy 6:12
Restitution	When a man or woman commits any of the sins that men commit by breaking faith with the Lord, and that person is guilty, he shall confess his sin which he has committed; and he shall make full restitution for his wrong, adding a fifth to it, and giving it to him to whom he did the wrong.	Numbers 5:6-7, RSV
Involvement	Go home to thy friends, and tell them how great things the Lord hath done for thee.	Mark 5:19

of their theologies with gusto, wit, and venom."[4] (Whether these are really secular concepts may be open to question.) _Yes!_

Mowrer's formulations are at least parallel with many biblical statements made long before the so-called "secular concepts" were enunciated. In the accompanying chart are to be seen some biblical statements which at least coincide with the affirmations of integrity therapy. These statements and Scripture verses are set out with the knowledge that "the devil can quote the Scriptures for his own purposes" and with the realization that proof texts don't always tell the story. Nevertheless, it must be obvious to the open-minded reader that integrity therapy follows not only the letter but also the spirit of the Bible.

It may be that the church will have to work for new vitality in the small groups within its fold. The "growing up" process in organizational experience leading to consolidation, bureaucracy, and decadence is constantly with us. Some of our large churches are like business corporations over which the minister presides as president, with the members the stockholders to whom an occasional report is made. The priesthood of all believers is little more than mockery. Although the church may exist primarily for the worship of God, it also has a ministry to man. "Bear ye one another's burdens, and so fulfil the law of Christ."[5]

There is no magic in a small group meeting as such. It must have a purpose. Some discussion groups easily degenerate into "a mutual interchange of ignorance." An integrity therapy group focuses on people where they are facing their difficulties and problems and gives them opportunities for openness in a situation not too far removed from the *koinōnia* of the early church.

Integrity therapy may call for a new elucidation of the relationship of faith and action in Christianity. One of Mowrer's complaints against Protestantism concerns what Bonhoeffer calls "cheap grace." He feels that much of the emphasis on justification by faith implies that having believed, the individual has no responsibility to act. However, a closer examination will show that even though Paul has often been held responsible for propagating this idea, he obviously was also opposed to "cheap grace." He cried out, "Shall we continue in sin, that grace may abound? God forbid."[6] "Work out your own salvation with fear and trembling."[7] James makes a similar emphasis, "Be ye doers of the word, and not hearers only, deceiving your own selves."[8] "What doth it profit, my brethren, though a man say he hath faith, and have not works? can faith save him?"[9] "Faith without works is dead."[10]

Faith should have a certain dynamic. The famous "faith chapter" in the epistle to the Hebrews, after a definition of faith, goes on immediately to present its roll call of the heroes of faith. It is a chapter of tumultuous activity. The heroes of faith who, "through faith subdued kingdoms, wrought righteousness"[11] were involved in life and the doings of their fellows. This dynamic faith concept must be rediscovered by the church.

Mowrer's theories have been called an "unfinished symphony" because they leave out the forgiveness which comes from God through Christ. If we are to put this doctrine back into its context, we will have to make the New Testament emphasis on the place of a changed life and behavior pattern in which the individual, experiencing forgiveness through faith, steps up to new heights of behavior and service to his fellowman.

If these ideas are really put into practice by Christians, both ministry and laity, the carpenter of Galilee may again manifest himself as he did to the selfish, grasping tax-gatherer, toward whom he took the initiative and evoked the response of confession, penance, and restitution, "Behold, Lord, the half of my goods I give to the poor; and if I have taken any thing from any man by false accusation, I restore him fourfold."[12] Following in the Saviour's steps, we, too, may hear his commendation, "This day is salvation come to this house."[13]

EPILOGUE

In response to an enthusiastic report of results of our integrity therapy group activity, Dr. Mowrer replied, "This is a potent piece of truth." The expression startled me. A helping technique may be but truth! The statement set me to asking, like Pilate of old, "What is truth?"

There can be no gainsaying the fact that few events in man's earthly pilgrimage are more mysterious and perplexing than his experiences of guilt. Freud confronted the difficulty and spoke of guilt as "the most important problem in the evolution of culture." As Reik has observed, the really astonishing thing is that so little has been done to research and understand the problem. The result has been that many old ideas which have been unthinkingly passed on and perpetuated are in need of critical reappraisal.

Even as at least one group of serious researchers has started on a process of reassessment of guilt, it has become obvious that there are some fairly simple logical explanations of what is taking place in an operation long shrouded in mystery. One would imagine that in accordance with the "law of parsimony" the simple theory would be attractive to students of personality. The surprising criticism is that integrity therapy oversimplifies both religion and psychology. It might well be that they both need simplifying.

Religion is seldom at its best in the complexities of theological hairsplitting or academic disputation. (The best aspects of "pure religion" are often seen in the lives of people dedicated to helping their fellowmen and women, while the theologians' musty tomes gather dust on library shelves.)

Psychology has fared little better at the hands of the savants with their penchant for fashioning words and struggling to be recognized as "scientific." In one seminar the trainee counselors reported on systems of psychotherapy. Engaged in counseling themselves, their assignment was to present a picture of the operational procedures of psychotherapists functioning within different theoretical frameworks. To discover a step-by-step description of any theory was practically impossible. And this despite the fact that psychotherapy is probably the most practical expression of psychology.

No one who has struggled through Mowrer's massive volumes on learning theory or his technical articles scattered through learned psychological journals could accuse him of shallowness of thought. If surprise there be, it is that this academician should have produced a theory so simple that, as a physician remarked, "It makes sense to ordinary people."

While Freud is generally credited with popularizing the concept of the unconscious, there was one area of unconscious functioning which puzzled him. In a communication to Reik, Freud noted, "The darkness which still covers unconscious guilt feelings does not seem to be lighted by one of the discussions about it. The complication only increases."

It is not without significance that one of Mowrer's most recent papers is "Conscience and the Unconscious." Much of the theorizing of integrity therapy has deliberated on the unconscious functioning of the superego. The darkness is rapidly being illumined and will hopefully be finally dispelled.

Integrity therapy is certainly nothing new. There are some unchanging principles of human reaction. Sometimes garnered after years of search, the precious pearls of wisdom are allowed to slip from us and must be periodically rediscovered.

Elements of integrity therapy are to be found in the earliest recorded experiences of man. Adam in the Garden of Eden reaped the penalty of irresponsibility and deception. The story of man tells us secretiveness and evasion have as surely cursed him as openness, accepting responsibility and commitment to life have brought deliverance and meaning to the human quest.

NOTES

Chapter 1

1. William Glasser, *Reality Therapy* (New York: Harper & Row, 1965), pp. 42-43.
2. *Ibid.*, p. 55.
3. *Ibid.*, p. 60.
4. *Ibid.*
5. O. Hobart Mowrer, *The Crisis in Psychiatry and Religion* (Princeton, N. J.: D. Van Nostrand Co., 1961).
6. ————, *The New Group Therapy* (Princeton, N. J.: D. Van Nostrand Co., Inc., 1964).
7. David R. Mace, "Marriage Guidance in Britain," *Southern Baptist Family Life Education*, V (April, May, June, 1959), 4.

Chapter 2

1. Robert J. Havighurst and Hilda Taba, *Adolescent Character and Personality* (New York: John Wiley & Sons, 1949), p. 194.
2. John Dewey, *Human Nature and Conduct* (New York: Henry Holt & Co., 1922), p. 315.
3. Lester A. Kirkendall, *Premarital Intercourse and Relationships* (New York: The Julian Press, 1961), pp. 5-8.
4. *Ibid.*
5. Anton Boisen, *The Exploration of the Inner World* (New York: Harper & Bros., 1936), p. 177.
6. *Ibid.*, p. 178.
7. Romans 7:7, RSV.
8. Robert C. Leslie, *Jesus and Logotherapy* (Nashville: Abingdon Press, 1965), p. 15.
9. James C. Coleman, *Personality Dynamics and Effective Behavior* (Chicago: Scott, Foresman & Co., 1960), pp. 306-7.
10. David Belgum, *Guilt: Where Psychology and Religion Meet* (Englewood Cliffs, N. J.: Prentice-Hall, 1963), p. 49.
11. Boisen, *op. cit.*, p. 55.
12. Lou Gottlieb, "The Unfortunate Miss Bailey," *The Kingston Trio,* Hansen Publication, Inc. Used by permission.
13. Boisen, *op. cit.*, pp. 56-57.

14. Lucy Freeman, *Before I Kill More* (New York: Crown Publishers, 1955), p. 23.

15. L. Salzman and J. Masserman, *Modern Concepts of Psychoanalysis* (New York: Citadel Press, 1962), p. 38.

16. Percival M. Symonds, *Dynamics of Psychotherapy* (New York: Grune Stratton, 1957), II, 396.

17. Lewis R. Wolberg, *The Technique of Psychotherapy* (New York: Grune & Stratton, 1954), p. 678.

18. Boisen, *op. cit.*, p. 5.

19. Anton T. Boisen, *Out of the Depths* (New York: Harper & Bros., 1960), p. 197.

20. Mowrer, *New Group Therapy*, pp. 184-85.

21. *Ibid.*

22. *Ibid.*

23. Erik H. Erikson, *Young Man Luther* (New York: W. W. Norton & Co., 1958), p. 19.

Chapter 3

1. James B. Donovan, *Strangers on a Bridge* (New York: Popular Library, 1964), p. 233.

2. Glasser, *op. cit.*, pp. 13-14.

3. Paul Tournier, *Guilt and Grace* (London: Hodder & Stoughton, 1962), p. 10.

4. John C. McKenzie, *Guilt: Its Meaning and Significance* (New York: Abingdon Press, 1962), p. 48.

5. Tournier, *op. cit.*, p. 10.

6. O. Hobart Mowrer, "Why I Don't Drink," *The Discoverer*, I, No. 4 (October, 1964), 7-8.

7. Quoted in McKenzie, *op. cit.*, p. 81.

8. Donovan, *op. cit.*, p. 232.

9. Tournier, *op. cit.*, p. 176.

10. McKenzie, *op. cit.*, p. 23.

11. Glasser, *op. cit.*, p. 77.

12. *Ibid.*, p. 79.

Chapter 4

1. Edward A. Shields, Robert K. Merton and Paul K. Lazarsfeld, "Primary Groups in the American Army," *Continuities in Social Research* (Glencoe, Illinois: The Free Press, 1950), p. 25.

2. Calvin S. Hall and Gardiner Lindzey, *Theories of Personality* (New York: John Wiley and Son, 1957), p. 134.

3. Elizabeth K. Nottingham, *Methodism and the Frontier* (New York: Columbia University Press, 1941), p. 110.

4. Walter Houston Clark, *The Oxford Group* (New York: Book-man Associates, 1951), p. 168.

5. *Alcoholics Anonymous* (New York: Alcoholics Anonymous World Services, Inc., 1955), pp. 59-60.

6. *Ibid.*

Chapter 5

1. C. G. Jung, *Modern Man in Search of a Soul* (New York: Har-court Brace & Co., 1933), pp. 31-32.

2. William James, *The Varieties of Religious Experience* (New York: Longmans, Green & Co., 1929), pp. 462-63.

3. A. A. Brill, *Basic Principles of Psychoanalysis* (New York: Wash-ington Square Press, 1960), p. 7.

4. *Alcoholics Anonymous*, pp. 72-73.

5. Robert A. Harper, *Psychoanalysis and Psychotherapy* (Engle-wood Cliffs, N. J.: Prentice Hall, 1959), p. 6.

6. Albert Ellis, *Homosexuality: Its Causes and Cure* (New York: Lyle Stuart, 1965), pp. 96-97.

7. Theodor Reik, *Myth and Guilt* (New York: George Braziller, 1957), p. 380.

8. Boisen, *Out of the Depths*, p. 100.

9. Exodus 21:23-25.

10. Numbers 5:6-7, RSV.

11. Leviticus 6:4-5, RSV.

12. James G. Emerson, Jr., *The Dynamics of Forgiveness* (Phila-delphia: The Westminster Press, 1964), p. 76.

13. John R. Scott, *Confess Your Sins* (Philadelphia: The West-minster Press, 1964), p. 32.

Chapter 6

1. Ivan M. Mensh, "Psychopathic Conditions, Addictions, and Sex-ual Perversions," *Handbook of Clinical Psychology* (New York: McGraw Hill Book Co., 1965), p. 1064.

2. Joseph A. Shelly and Alexander Bassin, *Daytop Lodge—A New Treatment Approach for Drug Addicts*, reprint from *Corrective Psychiatry*, Vol. II, No. 4.

3. *Ibid.*, p. 190.

4. *Ibid.*, p. 191.

5. *Ibid.*, p. 193.

6. *Ibid.*

7. *Ibid.*, p. 192.

Chapter 7

1. Carl R. Rogers, *Counseling and Psychotherapy* (Cambridge: Houghton Mifflin, 1942), p. 31.

2. Mowrer, *New Group Therapy*, p. 101.

3. Phillip A. Anderson, "Ministering to Troubled People," *The Chicago Theological Seminary Register*, February, 1965, p. 9.

4. Reuel L. Howe, *The Miracle of Dialogue* (New York: Seabury Press, 1963), p. 37.

5. Anderson, *op. cit.*, p. 9.

Chapter 8

1. Helen Joseph, "The Mask," *Saturday Review*, August 13, 1932.

2. Luke 12:1-3, RSV.

3. Proverbs 28:13.

4. Sydney M. Jourard, *The Transparent Self* (New York: D. Van Nostrand, 1964).

5. Joshua 7:19.

6. Matthew 3:6.

7. Acts 19:18-19, RSV.

8. James 5:16.

9. Thomas M. Lindsay, *A History of the Reformation* (Edinburgh: T. & T. Clark, 1959), p. 216.

10. Roland H. Bainton, *Here I Stand* (New York: The New American Library of World Literature, 1950), p. 106.

11. Scott, *op. cit.*, p. 12.

12. O. John Rogge, *Why Men Confess* (Edinburgh: Thomas Nelson & Sons, 1959), p. 155.

13. *Ibid.*

14. Catherine Marshall, *A Man Called Peter* (New York: Fawcett World Library), p. 155.

15. Jung, *op. cit.*, p. 35.

Chapter 9

1. Genesis 4:7.

2. Jourard, *op. cit.*, p. 4.

3. Galatians 6:2.

4. Galatians 6:5.

5. Perry London, *The Modes and Morals of Psychotherapy* (New York: Holt, Rinehart, & Winston, 1964).

6. *Ibid.*, p. 139.

7. James, *op. cit.*, p. 31.

8. O. Hobart Mowrer, "Alone But Not Alone," unpublished paper.

9. Frederick C. Thorne, "The Etiology of Sociopathic Reactions," *American Journal of Psychotherapy*, April, 1959, pp. 319, 330.

10. David Abrahamsen, *Road to Eternal Security* (New York: Prentice Hall, 1958).

11. Richard A. Cloward and Lloyd E. Ohlin, *Delinquency and Opportunity* (Glenco: The Free Press of Glencoe, 1961), p. 132.

12. Thorne, *op. cit.*

13. "Homosexuals Can Be Cured," *Time*, February 12, 1965, p. 46.

14. Boisen, *Exploration of the Inner World*, p. 179.

15. Glasser, *op. cit.*, pp. 128-29.

16. Genesis 4:12.

17. Genesis 4:13.

Chapter 10

1. Ellis, *op. cit.*, p. 133.

2. Rogers, *op. cit.*, p. 29.

3. Mowrer, *New Group Therapy*, p. 101.

4. Robert C. Leslie, *Jesus and Logotherapy* (Nashville: Abingdon Press, 1965), p. 76.

5. John Atkins, *Arthur Koestler* (New York: Roy Publishers, 1956), p. 91.

6. *Ibid.*, p. 95.

7. Glasser, *op. cit.*, p. 129.

8. Lindsay, *op. cit.*, pp. 216-17.

Chapter 12

1. Boisen, *Out of the Depths*, p. 186.

2. Philip A. Anderson, "The Implication and Challenge of O. Hobart Mowrer's Position for the Church and Its Ministry," an unpublished paper.

3. Mowrer, *New Group Therapy*, p. 162.

4. London, *op. cit.*, p. 135.

5. Galatians 6:2.

6. Romans 6:1-2.

7. Philippians 2:12.

8. James 1:22.

9. James 2:14.

10. James 2:26.

11. Hebrews 11:33.

12. Luke 19:8.

13. Luke 19:9.

INDEX